P9-CDK-583

Praise for *How to Be You*

"This is a book for anyone who feels out of place. Jeffrey will help you trust that your feelings are legitimate, and the life you want is just around the corner. Find peace with yourself, and let Jeffrey teach you *how*."

> —Sarah Lohman, author of *Eight Flavors*
> and *Four Pounds Flour*

"The luminous Jeffrey Marsh gifts us all with *How to Be You*. Expanding from their sparks of online affirmations into an enlightening how-to manual for self-discovery and delight, Jeffrey guides us through the creative, ever-evolving process of understanding and accepting ourselves. Ultimately, they remind us the best person we can become is our self."

> —Amy Deneson, writer and activist, GLSEN

"Jeffrey Marsh has created an inspiring guide to help us all discover and honor our 'best selves.' Through a combination of beautiful personal stories and interactive activities, infused with inimitable style and thoughtful insights, Jeffrey's book encourages us all to 'just be, and live our lives with dignity.'"

> —Daryl Roth, Tony Award–winning theater producer of
> *Kinky Boots* and *The Normal Heart*

HOW
TO BE
YOU

STOP TRYING TO BE SOMEONE ELSE
AND START LIVING YOUR LIFE

JEFFREY MARSH

A TarcherPerigee Book

tarcherperigee

An imprint of Penguin Random House LLC
375 Hudson Street
New York, New York 10014

Copyright © 2016 by Jeffrey Marsh
Penguin supports copyright. Copyright fuels creativity, encourages diverse voices,
promotes free speech, and creates a vibrant culture. Thank you for buying an authorized
edition of this book and for complying with copyright laws by not reproducing, scanning,
or distributing any part of it in any form without permission. You are supporting writers
and allowing Penguin to continue to publish books for every reader.

Illustrations by Danny Coeyman

Tarcher and Perigee are registered trademarks, and the colophon is
a trademark of Penguin Random House LLC.

Most TarcherPerigee books are available at special quantity discounts for
bulk purchase for sales promotions, premiums, fund-raising, and educational needs.
Special books or book excerpts also can be created to fit specific needs.
For details, write: SpecialMarkets@penguinrandomhouse.com.

LIBRARY OF CONGRESS CATALOGING-IN-PUBLICATION DATA
Names: Marsh, Jeffrey, author.
Title: How to be you : stop trying to be someone else and
start living your life / Jeffrey Marsh.
Description: New York : TarcherPerigee Book, [2016]
Identifiers: LCCN 2016000767 (print) | LCCN 2016008780 (ebook) | ISBN
9780143110125 (pbk) | ISBN 9781101993026 (ebook)
Subjects: LCSH: Self-acceptance. | Self-esteem. | Self-realization.
Classification: LCC BF575.S37 M366 2016 (print) | LCC BF575.S37
(ebook) | DDC 158.1—dc23

Printed in the United States of America
3 5 7 9 10 8 6 4

Book design by Elke Sigal

for Rick, *who has always seen the value in me and helped me see it in myself*

for Danny, *who has added his beautiful art and soul to this book and my life*

for Mom and Dad *for supporting me in telling my whole story*

and, of course, **for the love of my life, Jeff**, *who has always seen and honored the real me, even when I wasn't sure who that was*

This book is **dedicated to anyone who has ever felt like an outsider**. *Yes, you can sit with us at lunch.*

CONTENTS

INTRODUCTION

T his book comes straight from the heart. And it aims for the heart too. If I could offer a teeny bit of advice, it's not to shoot for understanding anything in here, but to shoot for seeing what resonates with what you already understand. I beg you to look for your own truth. What connects with your own life and with the world as you see it? What zaps you right in the heart? I have endeavored to make so much of this book about your experience. I trust you deeply and I want you to trust your own truth of what we're going to talk about too. So you'll notice that each chapter has some kind of fun, challenging, enlightening, and delightful exercise or *experience* of the topic at hand. We are creating this book together and it is meant to be the manual on how to be you that you didn't get while growing up. It's never too late to learn how to live a full happy life *as you*, and now's the best time to start.

One more suggestion before we get started. Repeat this book. Your understanding of the things in these pages will deepen and grow as you grow, so I've made it easy to repeat and reread it every five years or every year or every week. In this book, you will create astounding expressions of who you are, and build your own windows into how the world works. Who wouldn't want to do that again and again? Why not keep refining your idea of how to be you? So grab your pencil and crayons and enjoy yourself. Before we get into the heavy, joyful stuff, a little bit about me . . .

FARMLAND FANTASTIC

I grew up poor. By the time I realized the barn could be my theater, our farm was in decline. When I was old enough to help with chores, my family's farm was reduced to raising just a few animals and planting two crops: corn and soybeans. Mom had a rural farm joke she liked to tell people she just met: Did you hear that our bathroom caught on fire? Thank God the fire never reached the house! Like any good joke, it's an exaggeration, but it reveals how far down a dirt road we actually lived. I spent the first few years of my life without a street address and without any idea that there were other people like me (just an occasional mention of the "gay plague" on TV).

There was one place where I did feel totally like myself when I was growing up. Before I found community theater, I had a place where I didn't have to worry about being punished and I could express myself as myself. There was a stage. Footlights. A velvet curtain, a packed crowd. All I needed to do was rearrange a few bales of hay and it would be real. The old barn could be my private dress-up theater. Expressing myself on the farm was always a bit complicated, but when I discovered the raised platform inside our abandoned barn, I could see a safe, private space to explore being a fab ten-year-old. It was a stage for self-expression. I started playing there almost exclusively. To be in that safe space was addictive, all that twirling, dancing, and even singing, feeling secure and whole. There was an old trunk I took from our attic to store odds and ends of skirts and gloves I found in thrift stores or got from friends. The shows were always glittery musical extravaganzas, hours on end of playtime dancing and romancing. While my older brother and his friends went hunting or played football, I brought Vegas to the barnyard.

I don't think Mom and Dad ever did find out about the barn. If they did, they didn't say. I know raising me couldn't have been easy. They both had ideas about how life was supposed to be for me, about what the "right" path was for me. Over the years I've come to drop the chains of wishing they were *my* idea of perfect. Maybe all children drag around ideas about how their parents could have done things better. But, of course, we're all doing our best.

At some point, around the time my mom suspected I was wearing her shoes, something became crystal clear: they couldn't possibly "love me for who I am" if they didn't *know* who I was. I realized this when I was eleven. It was time to come out to my mom. As the moment approached to tell her, I pictured myself triumphantly saying, "I have an announcement: I'm from Planet Spectacular! I have come to take over and rule, with Tom Cruise by my side!" All I could muster, though, in a creaking, changing voice, was a stammer that sounded something like "I think I like boys." There were a million more hidden, beautiful, heavenly, stuffed, and shamed parts of my story, but that tiny sentence would have to be enough for then.

Mom hit the brakes. I was scared. She was scared. We were driving home from church; I couldn't tell if my timing was impeccable or exceedingly unfortunate. She swerved off the road, perhaps with God on her mind (she was, after all, a Lutheran pastor).

"You can't say that! You're eleven years old. You don't know anything about that!" she said.

The ideas she had about me, the plans she had for my future, were all changing before her eyes. I would never be her version of the Perfect Son. I can understand how it would be tough to come to terms with that. It would take two more messy "coming out's" and seven more years of stammering to finally tell Mom that I wasn't going to be the world's idea of perfect—that I was going to be me.

Let me be clear: Mom loves me. Dad too. My parents are very supportive, even now. Mom has always fought for me. She is one of the strongest, smartest people on the planet. And back then she was told that who I was, how I expressed my gender, was her fault. She was told that this child she loved would lead a disease-riddled, psychologically disturbed, imperfect shell of a life. And without anyone else around to contend that view, it's not surprising that she spent a lot of time trying to correct what she thought was a terrible mistake.

Things did work out for the best. I see the perfection in my life today. Now I "dress up" as my life's work. I dress up because it's who I am. Several times a week I'm making glam music videos and sending out little messages of self-worth to millions of viewers. I love interacting with all kinds of people online. Messaging with folks who have their own entrenched ideas about being perfect, who wouldn't normally "get it," excites me the most. It proves that we're all more alike than we often admit. Everyone seems to be drawn to this message: there is nothing wrong with you.

I am often head over (stiletto) heels happy when someone doesn't even think about gender identity; they just look at my online presence and see their own goodness reflected back. Because the truth is, my personal journey may be unique to me, but ultimately we all struggle in some way with our sense of self, and when I speak to others, I'm just mirroring for them what they've always suspected deep down: they are great just how they are.

How to Be You

1

...

DON'T TRY TO BE PERFECT

Sorry! Perfection doesn't exist. Whoever taught you what it means to be "perfect" was making it up. Whoever taught *them* was making it up too. Perfection is a phony concept. It's a phony set of standards. Where did the standards come from? How did they start? You can't always be sure where your ideas about how you should be came from, but one thing to notice is that perfection often has a shifting definition. Over time, we as a society change our standards. And, yes, over time, you as an individual change your ideas about how to be perfect. What you think is the "perfect person thing to do" now may change in five years. It may change in five minutes. "Perfect" is a shifting, unclear, unreliable set of standards. Because of this, you will never meet the fake standards of perfection. This is awesome news! As soon as you give up the quest to be perfect according to some outside standard, you can start being you. Holy wow, I feel like that's so important I need to say it again. *As soon as you give up the quest to be perfect according to some outside standard, you can start being you.*

And there is a good reason you can't meet the standards. You are a *living, breathing human.* That's why no one can meet the standards. You are not some caged, bottle-able, sellable set of never-changing qualities. You are alive. And alive things change. It is constantly, always what you do. So you can either embrace change and get excited about it—you can even start to love it—or you can try everything to freeze yourself into a perfect set of standards. Good luck with that second one. You can't actually freeze yourself. But so many people just keep *trying* to freeze themselves; they keep trying to get to that perfect spot where they can be frozen and perfect and everything about their lives will work because they've done all the right things. Excuse me, but what kind of weird goal is that? Since when does trying to meet some passed-down fake standard of perfect equal a nice life?

It doesn't. It equals a life of constantly trying. You might keep striving for an idea of perfection for the rest of your life. Many people do. And it is not worth it.

You'll never get there. The standards for perfection shift and morph and climb so astronomically high that they are unattainable. Why spend your precious life trying to do something impossible?

It is not fun. Fun might not seem like an important criterion here, but why do something that is so unpleasant? If you could try to be perfect your whole life and have an awesome time doing it (even though it will never work), I'd say, "This is great. I'm so glad you're having so much fun. Yippee!" But of course trying to meet false and shifting standards is actually the setup to making a bummer of your whole life.

I have a question. What's the one thing about yourself that you were taught to hate? What's the biggest thing that you were taught is imperfect about you? Have you struggled with that thing your whole life? Have you tried to change and change and change that thing? Would you call trying to change that thing *fun*?

The same thing goes for your life in general. It isn't fun to try to control your circumstances; you can't try to "make perfect" outside events so that you can feel more perfect inside. Making your outside environment perfect is unlikely to work because you can hardly control *yourself*, let alone anyone or anything else you see outside you. Your idea of perfection is based on a faulty assumption: that you are separate from the world and can judge how it should be. What if life has its own kind of perfection in it without your "help"? What if you, just as you are, are part of life's perfection?

THE PERFECT PROM THAT ALMOST WASN'T

One clear spring morning on our family farm in York County, Pennsylvania, I received a phone call. "I'm scared. I can't go," said a shaky, squeaking voice on the other end of the line. With that, my perfect prom was ruined.

I had come out as gay just a few months before. At the time, I felt a lot more complicated than "gay," but that moniker would have to do for then. It was vulnerable to come out, and so I thought that controlling everything else in my life and making everything else "perfect" would help me feel stable and capable. I wanted the perfect prom. There was this one tall, handsome boy in the only LGBT support group near our rural town. He was bad, a rebel. He had an earring! And, va-va-va-voom, he had a beard. Well . . . actually, it was a patchy, fuzzy beardlike conglomeration in his facial area, but it seemed like a beard to me! This was love. Looking back, I see it was radical (and generous) for Mom and Dad to drive me an hour each way to attend a gay-positive teen discussion group. It was even more radical for me to ask my rebel crush to come to prom at my ultra-conservative country high school. I would show the kids at school, I thought, because we would be perfect together. When I asked my crush, he said yes!

I had a vision of how it would go: We would look ultrachic and every head would turn as we entered triumphantly. We would dance under the fake string-light stars to the Bangles' "Eternal Flame." He would kiss me, and we would live happily ever after. Cue the glitter and balloons raining down on us.

When I heard my crush's voice on the phone that morning, though, the perfect prom I had crafted in my head, the one where I was perfect, where he was perfect, where our night was *perfect, gosh darn it*, started to crumble. He was concerned that we would be in danger. Kids at school didn't like the idea of the two of us going to prom together. They had already made threats about what would happen if my crush and I showed up. I didn't take their threats seriously. I was too busy trying to control the night and make everything "just so." But my would-be date did take the threats seriously, very seriously.

It was the morning of the dance. He said he could not go. I was devastated. This forced change felt like a mistake and it felt like my fault. At the time, I couldn't see that he was scared. All I could think was that senior prom would be embarrassing and awful and *imperfect*. It was not what I had in mind. I just kept thinking that I had done something wrong. I thought that if I could have been more perfect, somehow, or if I could have controlled things better, maybe the night would have gone the way I wanted it to go and I would feel okay about myself.

It was sad. I had dreamed of being the belle of the ball at my senior prom, with my crush by my side. But instead, I went alone. I wore a drop-dead gorgeous satiny 1920s tux and danced the night away with my friends. Without the pressure of being "on" with my crush, I had freedom to let go and enjoy myself. After all, by senior year, everyone at least knew that I wasn't a straight man—that I didn't see myself that way. And everyone knowing that was a great relief. Although I wanted to, I didn't *need* to put on a big, fabulous perfect show in order to feel like me. I didn't even need a date to feel like perfection, I just needed to let the night happen.

For many of us, worrying about what others think of us is so important. It is funny that the social world of Spring Grove High School seems far, far away, almost like a dramatic book I read in English class. Nowadays, I can barely remember the CliffsNotes! All those popular kids I was so concerned about impressing, the people I was so concerned about making things perfect for, have vanished from my life. I could not say what any one of them is doing today.

That night at the dance was a new beginning for me. I realized that maybe having the perfect image wasn't so important. Maybe things do not have to be managed and planned to be perfect. Maybe it will all be okay; maybe you can even have a little fun while you shake off the expectations the world has taught you.

Hero/ine

Simone Biles is an American athlete who has become the all-around world champion in gymnastics. She has gone on to shatter records by winning a total of ten World Championship gold medals, prompting *USA Today* to say about her, "No one does it better than Simone Biles. Certainly not now. Maybe not ever." She is a symbol of perseverance, dedication, and strength. At the same time, it is clear that she is not trying to reach some fake idea of perfection. When she is asked for advice, she often says, "Just go out there and do what you do in training. And remember, *have fun*." Simone has come so far and achieved so much without worrying about being perfect or whether she will get a "perfect 10." In fact, the International Gymnastics Federation has done away with the idea of a perfect score. In 2006, they switched to an open-ended scoring system. The federation said they wanted to be more objective. The new system makes it impossible to achieve a total perfect 10 score.

Without the carrot of perfection dangling in front of her, Simone can focus on other goals. To this day, while continually rewriting the record books, Simone simply has fun in gymnastics. She is part of a group of athletes who work hard and train diligently while enjoying themselves. She doesn't let the idea of needing to be perfect affect her love of gymnastics.

Another way to look at perfection is to say that you are, in a way, perfect already. You get to make up the definition of *perfect*, right?

So why not include yourself as you are? In this way, if you are already perfect, you are not broken. It's a very new, shiny notion: you don't need to fix yourself because you are already a messy, gorgeous, perfect human being. You are free to be life's idea of perfect when you stop trying to fit into society's idea-of-perfect box. You are free from an old, hard standard of what it means to be perfect when you see how truly perfect you already are.

And actually, that brings me to a larger point: we will never be able to fix what isn't broken. It is frustrating to try to be perfect by society's standards because that is the process of attempting to repair something that is working fine as it is. It is frustrating to fix yourself, not because you are bad at fixing but because you are unfixable-beautiful just as you are. If you look at yourself from a loving angle, all of your supposed flaws and "imperfect" ways are just fine. In fact, your differences are what make you important and unique. If you were a "fixed" person who met all the fake standards, you would be the same as any other fixed robot people and it would all be so boring. Life would be boring. No variety. Fixed perfect people would think alike and act alike and all have the same hobbies and shoes. But people aren't like that, thank goodness, and it actually makes each of us perfect in a very real, true way. Because the ultimate perfection is in our diversity. It's already in you, being just how you are.

When you reject the notion of needing to become other people's idea of perfect, you can see many more possibilities for how to live. I am not saying it is easy. It will take practice, and it will take perseverance, and, yes, patience. Maybe you could experiment with it a little. You could do one or two things a day *purposefully imperfectly*. You would find out if the world will end or if everyone will reject you. There is one thing I know: none of the worst that you think will happen if you give up on society's version of perfect will actually

When you don't meet the standards, when you aren't the world's idea of perfect, how do you treat yourself? List the ways you punish yourself for not being perfect.

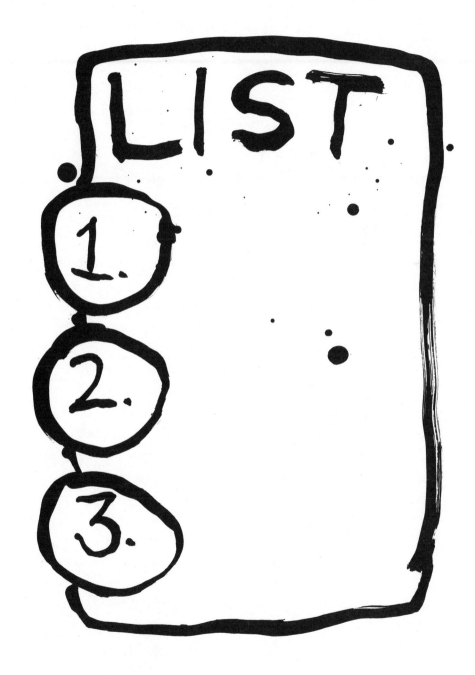

happen. In fact, once you get a taste of the freedom from *not needing to be perfect*, you can begin to *appreciate* your "imperfections." It sounds crazy, but one day you can start to *enjoy* not being that kind of perfect.

#DearJeffrey

How do I avoid trying to be perfect according to society's standards?

Once you understand the made-up standards by which society judges perfection, you can start to break the habit of trying to meet those standards. That's the fun part. Once your perspective has been broadened enough to see that it's a bogus system, you can start to play with that system.

Often, your sense of "imperfection" comes from the assumption, based on predetermined standards, that you have made a mistake. But this is only if you believe *mistakes are real.* In fact, there is nothing wrong with learning a lesson via your actions and their consequences. This doesn't mean you are imperfect somehow. There is nothing wrong with adjusting your life strategy as you encounter new information. There is nothing wrong with change. In fact, you can't seem to avoid change! Where you go "wrong" (not that it's a mistake!) is when you make changes *because of* your supposed mistakes. So many of us learned that that's the only reason to make a change: We did something wrong and now we need to fix it. But what if nothing is wrong in that way? What if everyone learns as they go? What if it is absolutely fine to:

1. try something

2. have it go a way you didn't think it would, and

3. try something else?

No idea of perfection. No standards to meet. If you call your first try, the one that didn't work so well, a mistake, you are more likely to feel imperfect and bad about who you are. And that is something you want to stop doing as soon as you can.

So, long story longer, play around with being imperfect! Experiment with the ideas around perfection. You can start chipping away at your own internal standards system. It can be as simple as wearing a color to work or school that you love but is widely considered by you or others as the "wrong" color for you. Or maybe you implement a new system at your job that isn't perfect but works for you. Mix it up. Change things. You can be like a scientist and study the results of your experiments. It can be as small or grand an imperfect gesture as you feel comfortable making, but you can always give purposefully "not living up to the standards" a try. You might even find you like it. When you give up on trying to be everyone else's idea of perfect, you can spend your life being your own version of yourself. You can spend time being *you*, or perhaps even . . . wait for it . . . you can spend time *enjoying* yourself.

IMAGINE YOUR

What kind of life do you want in five years?

Where do you want to be in ten years?

How about twenty years from now?

How will you feel when you have your perfect life?

PERFECT LIFE

Now go back and look over your answers from the last page.

Is there any way to feel the way you want to feel in the future right now?

Is there anything you can do in your life—right now, today—to feel the way you always wanted to feel in your perfect future life?

2

. . .

TRUST YOURSELF

When you were a kid, you received a kind of programming. From the time you were born, you were given cues and clues about who you are. You learned that you must act like a "good" person and not act like a "bad" person, and you even learned how "our kind" of people act as opposed to "others." Your parents and other adults told you: Don't do that. Don't touch that. Don't say that. Childhood has a lot of *don'ts*. And so you probably never got the idea that you are trustworthy, or that you belong here and the way you see the world is valid. And certainly no one told you that you are a superhero—no one whispered to you, "I know you have something to add to this world." No one told you that you have superpowers, and that the world needs you. Well, here's the truth: the sooner you trust yourself and trust your own worth, the sooner you can share your supergifts with the rest of us.

Superheroes are a great example of people who have faith in themselves. Caped Crusaders are aware of their own innate talents and abilities and they trust that they are adequate to any task. When I say "trust yourself," I mean two interrelated things. You can trust your heart to show you the impulses and special gifts and perspectives you can offer the world, and you can trust in your own adequacy.

Unfortunately, few of us were taught to trust ourselves. Everyone tends to internalize society's *don'ts* instead. You make your parents' jobs easier and start to parent yourself. You "don't" yourself. It's a more or less effective way to go from being a child to being an adult. Zen teacher and author Cheri Huber has said, "Parents are going to mess up their kids no matter what. They might as well do it in a way they're comfortable with." The programming you received is part of growing up and being socialized. It's part of maturing. And ultimately, that's okay. But in the end, you must reject a lot of your learned assumptions. And if you can't reject them, you must at least examine them—examine your programming, and throw away the idea that your inherent nature—who you are—is bad or untrustworthy. Throw away the idea that something about you needs to be changed in order for you to be acceptable. Your parents probably meant well. They were applying the lessons they learned as kids; they might even have been trying to change you for your own good. They might have thought that your intelligence or your sense of fun or your honesty would get you into trouble or get you judged. Your parents might also have been concerned that how you were as a child would get *them* judged. Chances are your parents taught you to stop trusting yourself. And so when you were eight years old you forgot how bold you were at two years old. You forgot how willing you were to try new things. You forgot how to naturally trust your own experience of the world. In short, you tried to fit in.

Because you wanted to fit in, you probably gave up much more of yourself than you needed to. You lost a lot of your bravery, your experimental approach to life, so that you could be accepted by other people. And was that process worth it? No. One hundred percent no. Depending on your personality, you might have eventually decided to rebel against all the training adults were giving you as a way to regain some of that natural power you felt as a kid. Maybe you did that in your teens. Or, instead of rebelling, maybe you assumed the adults were right and continued policing and judging yourself, just with more effort and enthusiasm. But either way, rebelling or internalizing, you were living a life *in reaction to* the way you were brought up. That doesn't strike me as a very free life—as a superhero kind of life. And I assure you: you are a superhero. Wouldn't it be nice to live like a fearless kid again, fight some bad guys and kick some booty, without feeling the weight of that unclear, worn-out set of *don't*s from your past?

Maybe you were a creative spirit born into a household that didn't know how to nourish such talents. Or maybe you were supersmart and your parents told you to stop "showing off." Or maybe, like me, you were simply unconventional and born into a time and place that required everyone to follow the rules. The thing that people around you tried to get you to change is a big clue about who you really are. In fact, that thing they wanted you to "fix" is likely your superpower. It's what you have to offer the world. It's what you're best at. It's what you're here for. You can trust those original instincts and talents. You can trust yourself.

If you were told as a kid that you were somehow "too much," rejoice! This will point you toward your superhero nature. With that admonition, "You're too much," you got a hint about what you are destined to offer other people. I was told that I'm just too much many, many times. I really didn't know what that meant until people started to get more specific: I was too feminine, too gay, too queer. I acted too much "like a girl." But don't you see? That's actually my superpower—I like to call it being fabulous. As far as I can tell, I'm here to help other people loosen up their ideas of identity and gender. I'm here to help people who feel restricted and held down by what it means to be a man or woman feel free. And I couldn't be of any help if I didn't trust myself. Being different—being too much, like people told me—is one of the best things about me. Can you imagine where I would be if I tried to ignore my feelings for my whole life—if I decided at some point that I couldn't trust myself and my experience? Where would I be if I decided that everyone else was right, that I am too much? I would have decided to trust the opinions of others over my own experience. And I would be sunk. My life would be small and horrible.

You were born with certain talents, certain ways of seeing the world, certain superinclinations—yes, they are superpowers—that may clash with the household you were born into. If they told you your personality was too big, then embrace that bigness. If they told you you were too shy, then celebrate your quiet introspection. Probably you were required to hide your superpower. The biggest problem with hiding your superpower, of course, is that you usually hate yourself in the process. You forget your bravery. You stop trusting yourself. Other people's words "You shouldn't be like that," in whatever context, become your own words "I am wrong for being like this. It's my fault."

Your hidden superpower might be the way you talk, or the way you express your feelings, or just *that you are willing to feel*. It could be anything that people encouraged you to change! And in the process of being asked (required?) to fix or hide who you are, you might have started to believe that your quirks, your special qualities, are faults rather than gifts. But here's the thing: superheroes don't live their lives based on other people's opinions.

CATCH AND KISS

I came into this world feeling really glittery and wearing (metaphorical) shiny gold bulletproof bracelets à la my idol, Wonder Woman. And I grew up in a house where a boy (their term for me, not mine!) was not supposed to be glittery.

By the third grade, I was already having crushes. Well . . . almost. What I did know by the third grade was that I very, very much wanted to hang around the school bully, let's call him J. I also knew that other people thought this was wrong somehow, that I shouldn't trust this part of me, that I should keep my infatuation a secret. I got the impression that I should have fixed it if I could have. But there was no "fixing" this attraction. J was assertive and, most of all . . . mean. He had a super low opinion of me. He was my archnemesis, in fact—but he was cute. How many superheroes have fallen for their villain in a moment of weakness? Why do we always crush on people who are so mean? Ah, sometimes to be young and in love means to go around saying, "Spit in my eye and I'll follow you around forever. Show no interest in me and I will break your door down with affection." Such is the story of me and J, Yin and Yang, Batgirl and Bane. We were meant to be together.

In the third grade when Mrs. Ellis would shove us out the door no matter what the weather, we had what she called "unstructured" time. One particularly bad winter, I can remember being layered up and clinging desperately with my tiny mittened hands to the doorjamb of Jefferson Elementary Schoolhouse. "Please don't make me go outside!" I screamed. But alas, Mrs. Ellis was always firm and kind. But mostly firm. "Everyone needs recess," she would say. I was clinging to the doorjamb for two reasons. It was cold outside. But also, I knew that J the bully would be waiting for me on the playground. Although I crushed on him, I feared him. J was always ready to taunt me over an enormous question. He loved to ask me again and again: "What side are you on? Which team: boys or girls?" He sensed I had something to hide and he also sensed his opinion meant every-thing to me. He was asking because every third grader (or what seemed like every third grader) would play catch and kiss. I guess the name says it all. The boys' team was responsible for both the catching and the kissing.

J was a world champion catch and kisser, a real star athlete of recess. And there I was, trying to hide, trying to fade into the jungle gym as best as I could. I wanted to avoid that inevitable question: which side are you on? Although I did not feel like a boy or a girl, I can remember being aware enough to know that, of the two choices, the girl's team seemed like the best deal. I wasn't 100 percent sure, but this whole "boys catch you, boys kiss you, I am the center of attention and all I need to do is squeal and run and pretend not to like it" deal sounded mighty good. Besides, I had to be on the girls' team. I was an excellent squealer. And mean ol' J was catching and kissing. That kinda cinched the deal.

But of course I couldn't say that I wanted to be on the girls' team. I couldn't trust myself and what I felt was true for me. I deeply cared what the other kids thought of me, and what J thought of me. And so I kept my mouth shut and I felt wrong. I felt bad for wanting to be on the girls' team. I wished I could be different, more "normal." I remember the shame. Somehow by the third grade I got the message that to choose the girls' team, to trust myself and line up on the girls' side against the red brick schoolhouse, would shock and disturb everyone, especially J (whom I very much wanted to please). Every recess was hellish because he would taunt me, intuiting that I wanted him to catch and kiss me, and often.

Eventually, the shame of hiding, and the pressure of the other kids' negative opinions of me, built up inside and pushed against the bottleneck lump in my throat. One day I had had enough, that winter day when we were all bundled up and shoved outside. I knew it was time to metaphorically rip open my button-down and reveal the gold lamé eagle breastplate underneath. It was time to trust myself. It was time to show strength. Driven by an adrenaline mix I like to call sheer terror plus desperation, I decided to try sticking up for myself. I did not answer J's taunts that day. Instead, I looked him right in the eye and wound my arm in a big circle, down, back, and over to bop J right on the top of his head . . . as hard as I could (which wasn't that hard because I still had my mittens on). It was the only thing I could think of to do! It wasn't exactly the smoothest superhero move, but J stopped in his tracks. He just stood there, blinking. I had stunned him. He did not seem able to process what had just happened. In that moment, he stood there frozen and blinking, with mind gears grinding, and I ran. I ran fast. If I had had the power to fly, I would have flown.

Recesses were different after I stood up to my nemesis. J did not terrorize me nearly as often. He sensed a new confidence in me, a new faith in myself. I didn't realize it then, but I was coming to trust my true strength. It was the strength of not having to make the choice society demanded. It was the strength of a conviction that I belonged on both the girls' and the boys' teams, and I could love that fact. Like any good superhero story, I was learning a big lesson: the thing that seemed like my greatest defect, my biggest flaw, was my greatest source of power. What some people considered my biggest weakness would turn out to be my biggest strength.

I used to think "unconventional" people like me are supposed to feel tortured. We're supposed to have dramatic bouts of self-hate, and disturbing dreams of never being good enough. I did have some of that, actually. But that was only the pain of not trusting my own experience of life. I had an idea of what was true for me and it seemed like I was being hated for something that I couldn't change. As I look back on my life, I see many triumphs. And you have triumphs too. Maybe your process is less about *becoming* a superhero and more about trusting the superpowers that are already inside you. The tricky part is learning to look at yourself in a new way. Can you take off the self-hate goggles and see yourself less as "becoming acceptable someday" and more as "always was and always will be acceptable"? Can you even go beyond seeing yourself as acceptable to seeing yourself as a hero? Like any hero, you have that quality that makes you different, the thing you think is tragic but is actually glorious.

#DearJeffrey

How are you so confident in life?
How can I be confident?

The confidence question is the most common one I get across all social media, and it's confession time: I'm not confident. At least, I don't always *feel* confident. But I suspect that when people ask me about being confident they are really asking me about trusting myself. "How can I be confident?" is another way of saying, "How can I trust myself?" If you learn to trust yourself completely, deep down, confidence isn't an issue anymore. Confidence comes naturally if trust is present.

Let me back up a second. The first step to developing a strong sense of trust in yourself is understanding that other people's opinions of you are almost always bunk—they are based on next to nothing. Most opinions are based on next to nothing! I don't ever feel sure about anything, and I bet you feel the same way sometimes. Once you get past the initial shock and fear of realizing that few of us know even fewer things, it is amazing. It is freeing. It is fun. Feeling sure about knowing something and learning to trust yourself are two different things. So do I trust myself more than I trust other people's opinions of me? I do now. And that, to me, is what is meant by confidence, trusting yourself. I couldn't have any confidence without trusting my own perspective on the world, instead of someone else's.

Choose one thing you think you'd like to be more confident about and take the time to look within yourself. If you want to feel more confident about reading things aloud at school or at work, say, you'd need to examine what you've already been taught about reading aloud, and decide what *you* believe about it. Does the ability or inability to read aloud mean something about you? Is it something that everyone *should* do really well? I'm not saying that uncovering and trusting what seems true for you automatically makes you confident, or that, in our example, it makes you excellent at reading aloud. To me, confidence is not attached to the *outcome* (whether you read well or not), it's attached to the *process*: How do you treat yourself while you're reading aloud? Can you trust your adequacy no matter what happens? If you know what's most important to you, it doesn't matter whether the reading goes well. This is hard to talk about because you were probably programmed to focus on how you perform in that situation. I'm asking you to focus on *how you do* what you do. That's trust. Take a big step back. See a bigger picture. Trusting yourself in every situation takes time and practice, and it takes focus. It's not about reading well, it's about staying in that trusting place with yourself while you read. That is the path of a superhero.

We tend to think of superheroines as *the other people*, these separate and superior superhumans who possess extraspecial skills and thoughts. That isn't true. They are just people who trust in themselves. Heroines are just like you. Heroes doubt themselves at first, just like you, *but they go ahead anyway.* Maybe what makes people seem confident is their ability to move forward even as they are building faith in themselves. They know they might make fools of themselves; they know they might fall flat on their faces. But they go ahead anyway, building trust along the way.

I see everyone as a hero. Life can be so tough sometimes. Other people's opinions can wear on you. Other people's hatred can make life feel very difficult for some of us. Anyone who can go through the challenges of dealing with others' negative opinions, of having their dreams mocked, or their feelings ridiculed, and still get out of bed, willing to do it again the next day . . . Whew! That person is a hero. *You* are a hero.

You need to trust yourself, and your own story. You need to add yourself to the list of heroic do-gooders because you have something to contribute. Maybe you don't wear a cape. (But, of course you could!) In your own way, though, you are brave. You have the ability to go ahead and do things you aren't sure about. You have the ability to go ahead and try things that other people think are stupid and wrong, but that you, in your heart, trust is right.

And aren't you lucky that you have the chance to do that? Aren't you lucky that you get this life, this chance, to learn to set aside the yuck and muck of other people's sometimes nasty words and do your best to live your life as fully as you know how? You don't need to be confident to do that. You just need to be a dreamer and a questioner, and have the willingness to trust that your experience—your way of seeing things—is valid. You need to practice trusting that you are worthy.

How do I know you can trust yourself and your instincts? Because I've been through it myself. When I was grow-ing up, everyone I knew (adults and kids alike) was trying to get me to suppress my natural qualities—my "too much-ness." They tried everything! They called me names, they threatened me, they used violence and emotional abuse, all to get me to change. And thank goodness I couldn't change. I tried for years, but I was horrible at pretending to be what I thought they wanted. You know what I learned from all this? Even if it seems like the whole world is against you, you've got to trust yourself. Even if no one else will honor you, you must honor what your truth is in any given moment.

I've talked a lot about how listening to other people's opinions of you is dangerous, but I haven't talked very much about how learning to trust yourself is a sublime and spectacular experience. Beginning to see yourself as worthy and trustworthy is the start of something beautiful. Why? Because you can finally let go. You don't need to spend all your time trying not to be too much. You can relax. You can feel safe. You deserve that. Everyone deserves that.

How do you do it? Step by step. Day by day. I sure wish there were a pill to take or a switch to flip and you would automatically see your value. But superpowers are sometimes hidden. Sometimes it takes experimenting. Often it takes time. What tiny thing can you do today to build that faith in yourself? What can you do today to practice seeing the best in you? For the longest time I've had a note in my phone listing things I've done that make me proud. I list the ways that I've showed up and been trustworthy. You might list your talents, or the fun things you add to other people's lives. Trusting that you belong here, that you add value to the world, is a process, and a practice, and it is so worth it.

It is also essential for having a happy life. Trusting yourself is the way to claim the life you've always been waiting for. I think when most people long for something (like longing to be confident), underneath is a longing for that trusting relationship with themselves. They long to see themselves as adequate. And that's what faith in yourself gives you—a steady relationship with yourself—a steady connection to the best parts of you. You get to let go and, well . . . trust that everything will be okay.

Hero/ine

When the DC Comics character Wonder Woman was created in 1941, the role of women in society was changing. Up to that point, many women were taught not to trust themselves. They were taught that other people's opinions of them—what their mother or their husband thought—were more important than their own opinion of themselves. The United States was at war, and Wonder Woman's creator, William Moulton Marston, sought to give America a new kind of superhero. He wanted to create a dependable, confident character who would triumph over evil not with violence—but with love. Marston's wife suggested he make the new hero a woman. Wonder Woman was born.

Although she is referred to as Amazonian, Wonder Woman is often viewed as thoroughly American. Because of this, she helped to ease societal tensions as women entered the work-force and began to trust that they could do the same work as the men they replaced who were fighting World War II. Wonder Woman is powerful, glamorous, and smart, and although she does use a lasso of truth and indestructible bracelets, it is often her ingenuity and her reliance on her own innate talents that save lives.

Wonder Woman is a model for the power of trusting yourself. In fact, Marston was clear about his intentions from the beginning: "Frankly, Wonder Woman is psychological propaganda for the new type of woman who should, I believe, rule the world."

Use this space to design your very own superhero cape. Draw, paste, paint. Remember, this is *your* creation. Make sure the colors and symbols represent your talents and superpowers. Show the evildoers of this world what gives you strength, the ways you're trustworthy, and what's most important to you.

#DearJeffrey

If someone has the same opinion of me that I have of myself, does that mean the opinion is true?

A big part of trusting yourself and your own superpowers is learning *not* to take the opinions of others at face value. Other people will always have a million opinions about you, but what's most important is your relationship with yourself. Other people's opinions are often not true. They are usually unsubstantiated. You can pick anybody in your life and I guarantee they'll have a different opinion than you about how everyone is supposed to live. If you were to talk to a random stranger from the other side of the world, you would quickly find out that their own opinions of what's normal or common are often totally different from yours. And so who can say which opinions are "true"? No one—that's exactly the point.

Now, learning to trust your own instincts is slightly different from having a good opinion of yourself. The kind of trust we're exploring in this chapter goes deeper. It's an experience. You don't just have an opinion that you're a *good person,* for instance; you commit to finding out that that's true. You commit to building trust in your goodness by looking for signs and clues and doing your best to see yourself clearly. That's different from an opinion!

Of course there are certain opinions that we have decided as a society and as a culture we want to support, certain ideas that we make into laws, for example. But notice that not everybody agrees with those! Not everybody thinks the same things are universally true. Not by a long shot. We live in a world of lots of differing opinions. And learning not to take too seriously the negative opinions of others helps to deepen your relationship with you. It helps you to naturally shine. It helps you to be the superhero you are.

But how do I know if someone else's opinion of me is true or not?

That's the thing! You don't. Wait. I should have said: That's the *fun* thing! When you realize that opinions can be wrong sometimes, you start to enjoy watching negative beliefs get negated time and time again. If someone has an opinion about you, you can look to your own experience to decide if there is value to it. Trust your own self-examination more than you automatically believe someone else's pronouncement.

Random "friend": You shouldn't have said that. That was stupid.

You: Hmmmm, it's interesting you say that. I don't think it's true, but I'm going to look at that for myself and I'll get back to you on what I see about it.

Along with clearing out the old beliefs other people have about you from the closet of your mind, you can start to organize the "keepers"—those beliefs that feel less like indoctrinated (but ultimately false) opinions and more like your own truths. If you start to develop a less serious attitude toward other people's opinions, you stand a bigger chance of noticing what feels less like an unkind opinion you were taught long ago and more like your truth.

But I hope you never find an *absolute truth*. We'll talk about it in a later chapter, but this kind of exploring and trusting is different from knowing exactly who you are and how you *should* be. Knowing tends to feel like the end of a story. And you are endless. I wouldn't want you to ever stop noticing what's going on around you and within you.

Truths can actually change with circumstances and time, and something you "knew" before can turn out to be an opinion you need to discard. The key is learning to trust yourself. If you can stay light-hearted and flexible through these changing truths, and remember not to judge what you find, you will never stop learning. I wish all of us would keep blasting away old beliefs and discovering new truths for the rest of our lives. I wish all of us would trust the truths we find.

If someone has a low opinion of me and calls me a name or says something bad about me, what if they're right? I mean, what if what they're saying *is* true?

That's fine! Let it be true. You could even, depending on how you feel that day, agree with them:

"You are such an idiot."

"Yup. That's probably right. Thanks for the update."

Again, other people's opinions are generally useless because they aren't based on anything universally true. One person is taught that everyone should put peanut butter in the fridge, and another is taught that peanut butter belongs in the cabinet. Where does that leave us? Is one family right for their cabinet opinion and another family wrong for their fridge opinion? Well, no. And when our opinion clashes with someone else's, it might be helpful to keep in mind that no one has all the answers. It's brave to admit that you aren't always right. And it's freeing to choose to enjoy the learning process and appreciate not knowing everything.

One of the big issues is that most people assume their own opinions are absolutely always right, but that's not the case at all. That's why it takes a hero to learn to trust the less obvious truths—

the deeper answers to life's important questions. It takes a hero to pause and breathe and really look for an inner wisdom. It takes a hero to commit to trusting that wisdom.

Of course, when you encounter a negative opinion from someone in your life that *matches* an opinion you have of yourself, things can get dicey. And it's worth talking about how that relates to trusting yourself and what to do when that happens. If there is a match between something negative you've always thought was true about yourself and someone else's opinion about you, it seems like the negative opinion is valid and real and true. As an example, say you usually think you shouldn't like yourself because you are too overweight. But then one day you start trusting a deeper knowledge; you think, *Where did we get these standards about what people's bodies are supposed to look like anyway? Why are people so obsessed with being thin? And what if I like the way I look? What if I like my body?* And then WHAM! a friend at school or work comes up to you and sneers, "You look like you gained some weight."

At this point I would recommend two things:

Don't ever talk to that person again. And . . .

Remember the great peanut butter debate.

Let's pretend that instead of the cabinet versus fridge argument, both families think peanut butter belongs in the fridge. That does not mean that the fridge is the *right place* to put peanut butter. Even if most people on the planet think peanut butter belongs in the fridge, it still doesn't mean that the question is closed and the fridge is the best place and now everybody in the world has to always put their PB in the refrigerator. I would encourage you to keep looking at the issue. What do you see about how your body is and whether believing that it should be different is a helpful or unhelpful belief for you? Trust your exploration.

I like the silly peanut butter example because it's a fun way of showing how unexamined opinions in general can be silly. If two people (you and your "friend") think you shouldn't be too fat, that does not make it true. And what does "too fat" mean exactly? Keep exploring and keep trusting yourself to find deeper and deeper wisdom about that. I know a negative opinion you have of yourself seems more real if someone outside your head says it, but really, people outside our heads are just as trained and just as prone to believe false, made-up opinions as we are.

LIKING LYNDA

Lynda Carter is one of my heroes. And when I was growing up, I wanted to be her. On my way to trusting myself, I trusted Lynda. To be more specific, I trusted Lynda's TV version of Wonder Woman. Lynda in tights and big hair was part of a sparkling schedule of glamorous, strong women on the limited TV stations I had growing up on the farm (only four channels!): Jeannie from *I Dream of Jeannie* was on at 2:00 P.M., Samantha from *Bewitched* was the star of the 2:30 slot, and Lynda's *Wonder Woman* came on at 3:00. After the ladies' shows, *The A-Team* was on, and I was out. I never liked to stick around for *The A-Team*. I was out the door and into the woods near our farm, running and tying on my flowing cape as I went.

This is what six-year-old me found out: If you want to be Wonder Woman, you need sturdy shoes, short shorts, and a bit of rope to lasso imaginary bad guys. You need self-assurance that your bravery is valuable. You need a long, shiny cape from someone's old Halloween costume that you persuaded your mom to buy at a thrift shop. You need to tell your mom that you want the cape so you can "pretend to be Superman." Growing up, it seemed like everyone wanted me to change myself. They wanted me to "man up" and act like what they thought of as normal. Eventually I learned to trust myself instead of becoming "normal." Through channeling my hero, I learned to open a channel to the real me. WWWWD? What Would Wonder Woman Do? I imagined that if I were her, I could deflect people's horrible words, their emotional bullets, with my indestructible gold bracelets.

So, yes, my outfit was incredibly en pointe. With my cape, I was ready to be a glam thwarter of any supervillain. Most kids play dress-up, I suppose, but I made it into an art. Playing in the woods around our farm was one of my only escapes. I could see I was different. I could see I was glam. It seemed that nobody else could appreciate that. I felt like I was on my own for most of my childhood. But it was okay because Wonder Woman was mostly on her own too, and she didn't mind it. She was too busy fighting the bad guys to feel bad for herself, or to get melancholy about all the lady friends she left behind in Themyscira, where she grew up. She trusted herself and her decisions. She had big hair and she didn't care what anyone thought of her. Not once (that I can remember) did she lasso-of-truth a villain just to ask, "Do you think I'm pretty?" or, "Can I sit with you at lunch?" I wanted her faith in herself, her heroic-ness. In a way, I used pretending to be Wonder Woman as a way to forget the pressure of figuring out who I was—and hiding who I was.

This ritual of running into the woods to take my chance at being Wonder Woman happened almost every day during the summer, and many days during the school year when I was "sick." Some days the teasing at school would be so bad that I would pretend to be ill and stay home to get a little booster shot of Wonder Woman confidence. During playtime, I always became women like Lynda's character: strong, clear-headed, independent. Wonder Woman is different from Superman. She is interested in more than just stopping bad guys through brute force. She wants to dress flashy and get at the truth, all while making the world safer. And I admired that.

At the time, I was dealing with a swirl of conflicting internal "truths." I was having trouble figuring out why the world wanted to change me and what that meant for who I was. My little life was unstable, to say the least. Back then, Dad wasn't around much and that kinda felt like my fault. I thought maybe he didn't want to be home with me because I was so different, so weird, so "not like the other boys." Tying on a cape and fighting bad guys made me a heroine—worshipped and loved. Playtiming as Wonder Woman gave me some stability, a chance to feel brave and sure and willing to stand up for myself, even if that was the opposite of how I felt inside.

A couple of years back, I started following Lynda Carter on Twitter, and I still follow her to this day. When she comes up on my feed, I remember playing in the woods, and the inspiration and confidence she gave me. I still have a special connection to her.

Why don't you trust your own value and your own deep truths? Why do other people's opinions of you seem to matter so much? When you were growing up, what your parents thought of you actually went beyond what was just important to you. Their opinions got linked to your survival. You could say your parents represented food and shelter. You are just figuring out the world when you're little, and you might end up linking the need to be seen as good by your parents with getting the things you need to survive. And then, unconsciously, as you grow up, you start to link everyone's opinion of you to your survival. Pleasing everybody and being popular might even feel like the most important thing in the world.

But being popular in other people's eyes isn't all that important. Learning to have a kind and trusting relationship is far more important. I'm not trying to be down on popular people, though. If you are popular, that's great, but no one needs to be popular to be acceptable, or to survive. You don't need to have everyone love you in order to love your life and have a good time. You don't need other people to have a good opinion of you to live a full and happy life. In fact, one of the biggest lessons you can learn in life is that it's impossible to make *everyone* love you, no matter how nice or generous or smart or hardworking you are. So eventually you need to focus on trusting yourself instead. You need to build that faith in you that we've been talking about.

Superheroes have jobs to do. And so do you. Your job is to try trust. Little by little, you can learn to reverse that programming that says what other people think of you is so important. One way to build this self-reliance is to spend time alone. You might even call it spending time with you. Take yourself on a date. Have dinner. Ask yourself questions and really listen to the answers. Be the loving companion you've always wished for. Find quality alone time to practice trusting your own inner wisdom. Turn off the electronics, maybe find some nature, and slow down. There is only one opinion that is vitally important: your opinion of yourself.

Imagine someone who has always been your hero. Pick anyone alive or dead, real or fictional—someone you admire for being strong and wise. Once you have a clear picture of your hero or heroine, write a dialogue with that person. Pick an issue that's been troubling you, or something you worry about, and ask your hero about it. You will be writing both sides of the conversation. Try not to predict or guess where the conversation will go, just do your best to speak honestly from the heart as you and as your hero. Use a separate sheet of paper if there's more to say.

Write a dialogue with your hero.

Remember: Your hero is a part of you. You wouldn't know what they "would say" if you weren't just as wise and trustworthy as they are.

3

· · ·

LEARN MORE
ABOUT YOURSELF

Want to know exactly how to be yourself? The first step is to enjoy the great news: you can't be anyone else. You are yourself and that's just how it is. Once you realize the impossibility of trying to be your cousin or teacher or Taylor Swift, you can settle into being you. But who is you? Maybe so many people have told you that you need to change, adjust, be a little bit different throughout your life that you feel a bit confused about who this "you" is that I keep mentioning. Well, more good news: I'm here to help. I want to help you get to know yourself so that you can actually start to get *comfortable* with yourself. Oh, sure, role models are great. There are many positive reasons to have role models. But in this chapter I want to encourage you to find out more about you. I want to encourage you to learn more about yourself because I'm betting that the more you learn about yourself, the more you'll start to see the role model you've always been. The more you see, the more you'll like this you we've been talking about.

So to get us started, a pop quiz! Okay. Okay. Don't mind that word *quiz*; it's just that "pop list of questions that are pretty cool" didn't have a real nice ring to it. You won't be graded for this. It's just time to sharpen your self-research skills. Each of the upcoming questions will give you a window into what's important to you and how you function and how you feel about some really deep subjects—ya know, fun stuff like that. On a separate clean sheet of paper (maybe in a notebook or journal) start by writing the number 1, then answering the first question. Keep going until you have an answer for all five of these questions. You don't need to go on for pages and pages; just a short paragraph for each is fine. Try not to analyze the questions or "get it right," just answer honestly and enjoy getting to know yourself. No one will see your answers so don't be afraid to keep it raw and off the cuff. When you are finished, keep the paper handy, so I can tell you a few things about what you wrote. Your extra-credit assignment if you so desire: have fun answering these questions.

Jeffrey Marsh's Old-Fashioned, New-Fangled, Get-to-Know Yourseeeeeeeelf Quiz

1. How would your ideal romantic partner or ideal best friend treat you? If you had someone who was very emotionally close to you, how would they act? What would they say to you? What would an ideal day with them be like?

2. What does sadness feel like in your body? Describe the actual physical feelings that go with being sad. Is the sensation heavy or light? Does it move and jiggle or does it feel more like something is stuck? Where exactly in your body do you feel it? Be descriptive and use as many adjectives as you can to describe how sadness feels, physically. If it seems like it would help, draw a picture of where sadness "lives" in your body. Now go back and answer these exact same questions about feeling happy.

3. Imagine you are all by yourself and no one else is around. Describe your usual experience. Is it lonely or glorious or something else altogether? Is it frightening? What is it like for you to be alone?

4. Currently, what's your biggest fear? What could happen to you that would be very scary?

5. What is one quality about you that people admire? When people tell you how much they love that trait of yours, how do you react?

Go ahead and answer them all. Do it. I'll wait . . .
(When you're finished, turn the page.)

45

Okay. Pencils down. Now that you've had a chance to answer the questions, take a few deep breaths. Congratulations! I hope you can feel how enjoyable it is just to discover new things about such an interesting person (you). As you read over your responses, I'd love for you to keep a few things in mind for each question.

1. *How would your ideal romantic partner or ideal best friend treat you? If you had someone who was very emotionally close to you, how would they act? What would they say to you? What would an ideal day with them be like?*

This is a really good indication of how you want everybody to treat you. And who could blame you? If everybody could be as kind and accepting as someone we're in love with or very close to, the world would be great indeed. This is also a clue as to how you wish you could *treat yourself,* and we'll get to that. For now, don't just notice your actual answer. Notice how you came up with the answer. How do you know what a romantic partner or a very best friend should say? Did you feel that they were something you deserve to have? Is there a sense in your answers that a close relationship like this is impossible for you? Maybe you felt like you had no interest in a close friend or partner at all. These are interesting things to notice.

2. *What does sadness feel like in your body? Describe the actual physical feelings that go with being sad. Is the sensation heavy or light? Does it move and jiggle or does it feel more like something is stuck? Where exactly in your body do you feel it? Be descriptive and use as many adjectives as you can to describe how sadness feels, physically. If it seems like it would help, draw a picture of where sadness "lives" in your body. Now go back and answer these exact same questions about feeling happy.*

Exactly where you feel your feelings is one of the most important things you can learn about how you tick. When someone asks you how you are feeling, do you always feel how you're feeling in the same part of your body? Maybe most of your emotions are in your chest or your throat. Your body is a part of what makes you you, and to know how it expresses and feels is a major way to see yourself. If you are like most people, you tend to spend a lot of time "up in your head," ignoring five sixths of yourself! Also really helpful to see are any judgments creeping into your answers. A big part of observing yourself is learning to do so as neutrally as you can or with a playful attitude, like a joyful scientist. Do your answers indicate that you have a certain opinion about sadness or happiness? Is one feeling better than the other? Did you see in your answers an idea of what you think about the feelings of sadness and happiness?

3. *Imagine you are all by yourself and no one else is around. Describe your usual experience. Is it lonely or glorious or something else altogether? Is it frightening? What is it like for you to be alone?*

Chances are, you were raised on distraction. TV shows blaring all the time, cruising on the Internet, you don't have time to look at (let alone learn about) you. This question will help you understand how you feel about looking inward. Do you hate it? Does it scare you? Is it something you love that you can't get enough of? There isn't a right or wrong answer here, it's just that how you approach this question, and how you approach the idea of being alone, gives you some clues about how you approach getting to know yourself. Spending time with you and learning about you are very much related. If alone time is something you hate, is it because you feel judged when you're alone? Or is being by yourself a chance to let go and sink into being true to who you are? Is it, maybe, a torturous, uncomfortable, desperate time? For you, it's probably some version of all of these, but however you feel about being alone is probably the same as how you feel about yourself in general. Consider how you might use some time in solitude to change and deepen your relationship with yourself.

4. Currently, what's your biggest fear? What could happen to you that would be very scary?

I talk a lot about fear in this book because it is such an important part of being a human being. In general, fears are your best indication that you are about to learn something big about yourself. If you are deathly afraid to tell someone, "Listen, it's not just that I like you, it's that I *like you* like you," for instance, there is a big chance that you might learn how much potential rejection you can handle— or how much potential excitement. Fear indicates that your horizons are about to broaden. You might be about to change your perspective on what you think you're capable of doing. Right on that edge of expansion, fear shows up. When it comes to learning about yourself, fear can be an indication of an area you probably want to explore. Of course, yes, there are truly awful things to be afraid of, like being killed or losing a loved one. But even those fears might hold clues to things you think you could never get over that you could come to terms with eventually. Learning about a fear in yourself is not a stopping point; it's an invitation for more "getting to know," for a deeper exploration. What does your fear say about you? Where are your current boundaries? Where might you expand a bit?

5. *What is one quality about you that people admire? When people tell you how much they love that trait of yours, how do you react?*

How you handle compliments says everything about you. Did your parents set out to teach you to be humble and actually end up teaching you not to have a very high opinion of yourself? Does it feel polite and nice to deflect or downplay a compliment? "Oh, no, it was nothing!" you say, hoping no one will notice that you really are as brilliant and smart and talented as they said. Or maybe you love getting praised. Maybe you say, "Thank you! I've always thought that about myself too," when people compliment you. However you react, and however you answered this question, there is no right or wrong way to be. To really drive home our theme for this chapter: you don't want to get into the habit of judging the things you find as you learn more about yourself; you want to practice enjoying the exploration.

Before we go any further, one more reminder not to judge what just happened. Do not judge your answers or how you came up with your answers. Maybe for a couple of questions you couldn't think of anything; maybe you feel like you didn't have a good or right response. *Give up those judgments.* Part of learning about yourself is learning to enjoy the process. Whew.

It's funny to think that you need an owner's manual, but chances are you grew up being told *not* to pay much attention to your inner life and *not* to notice how you function or even why you do the things you do. You probably got the message that self-examination might do damage or should be scary somehow. None of this is true! Knowing more about how you do what you do and some of the old (perhaps outdated) reasons you have for acting the way you act can be really helpful. It can lead to a lot of freedom in your life. And it isn't a contest. You can look inside just for the fun of it, just because you enjoy getting to know yourself like a friend would enjoy getting to know you.

I can hear you protesting. "That's so selfish! How can I put myself . . . *first*?"

It's a little-known secret that you *must* put yourself first, or to say it another way, there is plenty of time and attention and care in this universe for everyone, including yourself, and caring for yourself is the easiest and most convenient way to learn *how* to care. Care doesn't need to become about competition. It's not that once you start being kind and paying loving attention to yourself you will automatically be mean to or ignore others. As far as I can tell, the world isn't you versus them. You don't need to make a choice between caring about yourself and caring about others. Why not give love to *everyone*, including yourself?

And how do you care? You step back. You set aside everything you think you know about who you are and start fresh, like that clean sheet of paper from our exercise. And it sounds crazy, but you start to ask yourself questions and truly listen for the answers. Maybe nobody has ever really asked about your likes and dislikes and what you love before, so it may be hard going at first. Self-examination may feel awkward, but you are worth the try. Maybe nobody has ever really listened to what you have to say. Maybe nobody has ever really cared to know about your life. Maybe sometimes you feel like no one understands you. Learning more about yourself means being willing to understand yourself.

Let's try an experiment: Think of the meanest person you know. Do you get the impression that they take good care of themselves? That they feel heard? That they spend the weekend going on long walks alone and enjoying their own company? Nah. People are happy around others when they are happy with themselves. You are kinder to others when you are kind to yourself. Consider our little quiz from earlier as an example. I told you not to judge your answers because that isn't a very kind approach toward yourself. I know. It's weird to talk about approaching yourself, as if you're two people. But it does kinda feel like that: part of you speaks and part of you listens. The way to get kindness with(in) yourself is spending time being nice to yourself, spending time getting to know and (dare I say it!) getting to *love* yourself. It's not selfish. It may be the biggest, least selfish thing you do in your whole life. Loving yourself helps you love other people. When you get right down to it, there is little difference between you and other people. We all deserve love because we are all here, in this, together.

One tip I can offer is changing the way you talk about yourself. Don't use your speech to put yourself down. Stop saying "It's not important" when it is. Stop saying "Oh, it's nothing" when it is something. This will go a long way in helping you respect yourself enough to learn about yourself. When you downplay the things that are important to you, you cut yourself off from ever exploring your own wants and needs. This isn't something that you need to do in front of other people, but in private you can say, "Hmm, now, why is that so important to me?" If you make the unfortunate decision to view your own experiences and opinions as unimportant, you lose the chance to examine them. Who wants to study something unimportant? And as you find your interests more important, you can respect other people's interests too.

But it can also work the other way around. Giving love and respect to others also helps you recognize your own best qualities. You can't recognize a positive trait about anybody else unless you have already recognized it within yourself. You see that someone is kind, for example, and you know that only because you are comparing their behavior to your personal emotional and memory database of what it's like to be kind. You see kindness in somebody else because the concept is familiar to *you*; you recognize it from *within you*. Just like the dialogue with your superhero from the last chapter, you know what to say, you are the wise one. This is one of the best ways to learn about yourself! You see some awesome trait "out there" in someone else and then realize how you have that trait—how you are like them.

Remember that: you have the building blocks for all the qualities you see in others—courage and style and intelligence, or whatever else you are recognizing in heroes and want to learn more about in yourself. But of course that doesn't mean you should start comparing and finding yourself lacking. You don't actually need to wish for Wonder Woman's talent or bravery. She can simply be the inspiration to cultivate your own bravery. And you don't need to compare how you're doing with Wonder Woman—or with anyone else. There is a big difference between

1. recognizing everybody has value, and

2. deciding who is *more* valuable.

As you begin to learn more about yourself, as you start to uncover all the things you offer to the world, you must get stronger and more adept at dropping any comparisons. If you had a bunch of different flowers, would it really be necessary to compare one flower with another? There will always be someone else more or less intelligent, stronger or weaker, faster or slower, more or less talented, than you. Putting too much stock into feeling inferior *or* superior to anyone else is a waste of energy, and it opens the door to the idea that you *need* to judge and decide who is better. You're not Wonder Woman. *You're you.* And as soon as you give up on trying to be someone else, you can start to really enjoy being yourself.

I want to talk a bit about noticing other people's negative qualities. You may see meanness in someone else and then realize you have the capability for that inside you too. When you start learning more about yourself, you will need to accept your not-so-great qualities as well. These could be little things like the fact that you don't like someone you work with, or big things like you tend to hurt people close to you. The promise—the huge commitment—you need to make now and forever is to avoid judging anything you find as you get to know yourself. You want to avoid *any* hatefulness toward yourself if you can. Be kind to yourself: as kind as you would be to others.

Some more advice for self-discovery: Suppose you learn about a quality you possess that you were taught is flat-out wrong and unacceptable. Or maybe you already know of some supposedly wrong things about yourself: you fight, you get too dramatic, and you talk poorly about other people at school or work. Whatever it is, you may want to change it right away—to get rid of the "bad" thing about you. But you don't have to do that. There is an assumption in there that *you are bad* for doing these things, and that's not necessarily so. In fact, there is nothing wrong with you at all. You are just a person and sometimes you do things you'd rather not do. That's why I'm encouraging you to take a neutral approach—or a kind approach.

 Hero/ine

Lili Elbe was the first internationally known person who lived first as a man and then as a woman. She was also one of the first public figures in the twentieth century to be open about her unconventional gender identity, almost a hundred years ago!

Lili was born with the name Einar Wegener in 1882 and lived with a male identity while becoming more and more famous as a painter in Denmark. In her early twenties, Lili (then Einar) married a woman, Greta. Greta was also a painter and used hired models for her paintings of chic flappers and twenties-style women. When one of her models didn't show up one day, Lili stepped in and wore stockings and high-heeled shoes for her wife's painting. Over a series of months and paintings, Greta and Lili discovered that Lili felt most comfortable dressed as a woman. Not only is there no record that Lili judged this fact when she discovered it about herself, she began to celebrate what she had found, and to tell people about herself.

In 1930, Lili became one of the first public figures to pursue surgery to change her body to express her gender identity. This then-experimental surgery, along with four follow-up surgeries, eventually contributed to severe health problems and Lili died. Today she is remembered as someone who knew herself very well. She was a cultural pioneer and heroine for the modern transgender movement.

You can think of the advice you'd give to someone you love who might discover something about themselves that they don't like at first. Would you hate them because they found out a tiny thing they didn't like? Gosh, I hope not. Instead, you might offer them kindness as they grow, as they work with themselves, as they explore different ways of being. Practice giving yourself the same kindness and benefit of the doubt you would show to a friend.

You need kindness. Being yourself is a complicated idea. Learning about yourself is not easy. They are both simple phrases and we have all heard them before, but do any of us really know how to be ourselves and where to look to learn about ourselves? Do we know *exactly* what those phrases mean? There is one thing I do know: you won't be able to comfortably know and express all the parts of who you are until you *accept* all the parts of who you are. Judgment, blame, and shame are not helpful companions on a path to liking and learning. What I suspect most of us think about when we think of what it means to learn about ourselves is being comfortable with ourselves, feeling accepted in our own lives. And that is a great goal! But clearly, you won't get there by judging and hating, hiding and pretending. Also, I guess for a lot of us, knowing ourselves has to do with honesty. You may not actually know your deepest truths in any given moment. You may not have any clue about what is ultimately true for you. But to be able to be honest in your explorations *with yourself*, and even to be honest about how you may not know what's true for you, feels great. It feels real. It feels free. So go ahead and run head-on into an exploration of the parts of you that you've been told are unacceptable; peel off the layers of denial and shame and (perhaps wobbling at first) step out into the unsure, uneasy light of learning more about yourself.

If you feel unsure about taking the chance to see yourself from all angles, I'd ask you to consider the alternatives. What would you do instead of learning more about yourself? Let's see. You could hide and try to be the person you think other people want you to be. Okay, that sounds like fun (not). It's yucky to imagine a life devoted to being the fake you that other people are hoping you'll be. Actually, maybe you don't have to imagine this, maybe you're already trying to be what other people think you should be! If you ever have the choice between being honest—living a truth that seems right for you right now—and the (false) safety of pleasing everybody, you must choose being honest. That way, you can tell someone your truth. But you must know what you're being honest about as a first step. You must care to learn your truth before you can tell it. I would recommend the choice of freedom. I would recommend the choice of learning and embracing *and* telling. And once you get accustomed to the honest living that comes after learning about you, you will enjoy not having the pressure of needing to create a false image. You will have a sense of who you really are. When you have learned about who you are, you won't have to remember what you told to which friend and when, and you won't need to worry about how to hide from other people.

Yes, you might lose friends or even family when you learn something they don't like about you and tell it to them, but honestly, you might lose friends anyway. You might even lose someone very close to you that you care about by being yourself, but it's often worth it. Having all the friends in the world is fine, but nothing beats being able to be you in all parts of your life. It is an unequaled joy just to live openly, without the stress of trying to be someone else. There is a great connection between honesty and happiness and staying open and learning about yourself. You are looking for ultimate acceptance, to know that you are okay. And the *best* acceptance comes from inside you.

#DearJeffrey

What if I can't do this "learning about myself" thing? It seems so weird and different and selfish. And to be frank, it also seems kind of dumb.

Here's the secret of the universe: you can try something without liking it first. You can even *keep doing* something you don't like, just because you see it will have value down the road. Oh, sure, if something truly makes you unhappy, you ought to stop doing it. But I'm guessing you will find this habit of deeply looking into and finding out about yourself very fulfilling. So, to help, below is a list of all the excuses for *not* learning about yourself, some of which are included in this very question! This is a list of many of the things you might have been hearing inside your own head as you read this chapter. I present to you, all laid out, the resistance to self-knowledge, the false "reasons" *not* to explore you. Included with each is the quality in you that you will need to access in order to overcome each excuse, and a short description of how each one works. Follow along and take note of which ones you heard in your head while reading about this and which ones you usually say to yourself when you consider taking on any new project.

Excuse: This is dumb.
Quality in You: *Intelligence*

Calling something or someone dumb right out of the gate actually downplays your own smarts. Behind the assessment that something looks or sounds dumb on the surface is an assertion that you can't *find out for yourself*. You are intelligent. You can figure out if something is really dumb or not, and a snap judgment and label of "dumb" implies that you don't believe you can assess for yourself. This whole chapter may be dumb. It may not be dumb. I challenge you to find out for yourself. And how shall you find out? Keep trying the methods we're talking about!

Excuse: I don't feel like it.
Quality in You: *Willingness*

Just like calling something dumb, this excuse is rather shallow. Just saying "I don't feel like it" is supposed to be the end of the discussion and you won't go an inch toward doing the work to find out for yourself. What does "I don't feel like it" mean exactly? Is this referring to an actual physical feeling you get? Is it just a code for "I don't want to"? When you find yourself saying "I don't feel like it" and you leave it at that, you run the risk of missing out on something that might be quite cool. And you miss out for no real reason whatsoever. Again: try the process of learning about yourself, *then* decide how you feel about it.

Excuse: I'm afraid. What will happen?
Quality in You: *Fearlessness*

We all fear the unknown. And it's not how we usually talk about it, but there is a lot you don't know about yourself. You are a mystery. You are the unknown. And the good stuff in life is so often found on the other side of a fear of the unknown. You don't know what will happen, so your brain tends to come in and fill the unknown void

59

with the worst-case scenario. But it is very rare that the worst-case scenario actually ends up happening. So take a chance.

Excuse: I don't have time for this.
Quality in You: *Persistence*

What else are you doing with your life that's more important? Yes, it takes time to read self-exploratory books like this one. But not any more time than it takes to watch a video or listen to music. You have a lot of choices about how to spend your time, and spending at least some of it on yourself seems like a really good thing to me. You could say that your time represents your respect: what you spend time on, you value. Don't you value yourself? Don't you at least want to see if you can start to value yourself more?

Excuse: I can't do this. This isn't for me.
Quality in You: *Acceptance*

Ah, my favorite. I keep bringing up this idea of self-acceptance because it is so darn important for this kind of self-learning. That sentence "This isn't for me" cuts you off from a whole bunch of experiences and it cuts you off from yourself. As I keep pointing out, you will know only if you try, so I encourage you to find out if this kind of exploring is or isn't for you. Whether you end up deciding that this approach to learning about yourself is for you, you will at least have proved to yourself that you can do it. What I mean is, you will have exposed the phrase "I can't do this" for the lie that it is in the process of experimenting with knowing yourself a bit better.

VACATIONING

I was seven and I was a wiz at summer camp. Well, at one part of it at least. Let's be clear: I was made fun of a lot for being different. I was so different that *most* of the kids ridiculed me. But I did a little soul-searching and discovered I was great at anything that required performing, and the knowledge of this came in handy a few times. We had a contest at camp every summer, a talent show, and one summer I won the top award and the undying affection of at least four other campers. This is because these four other kids were my backup singers, and together we sang our way to summer camp fame . . . well . . . sort of. We were lip-synching, to be technical, so they weren't backup *singers* exactly. But the performance was glittering. We won partly based on talent and partly based on innovation. The curtain never *rose* on our performance because we just popped our heads out from under the curtain, upside down. We had drawn eyeballs, noses, and curly hair on our chins, to make faces on the other side of our mouths. And to look right side up, we topped it all off with little construction paper hats tucked over our jawlines. Sure, it probably had been done before, but never with such *flair*. Add some lip-synching to the *Sound of Music* soundtrack, and the crowd couldn't help but fall in love. That summer, I grew into the knowledge that I'm on earth to perform. I'm on earth to shine. I loved learning this about myself because it felt so freeing. It was liberating to just act crazy and make people laugh and be me, even if it was while lying upside down with a tiny hat on my chin.

Things always got complicated later in the summertime when there were things to learn about myself that weren't as fun—it was time for VBS: Vacation Bible School. This was a summer camp through my church, and it was a lot more conservative than lip-synch camp. Oh, I would make a friend here or there, which was great, but VBS was lacking in one essential element: where was the talent contest? People *were* given awards. People were praised, but not for their talent; they were praised for their loyalty to Jesus and their ability to recite Bible passages. *I wasn't nearly as good at that as I was at upside-down lip-synching Julie Andrews.* Jesus and I didn't feel exactly . . . friendly. I wanted to be. I wanted to fit in and be accepted at church, but early on a kid there told me that Jesus hated me. I needed to not be so different. I needed to not be so . . . myself. What did that kid at church mean? Who was I? What was the "different" he was talking about?

I've basically always been bright and, for lack of a better way to say it, exceedingly glamorous. I remember the day my rib cage got too broad to fit into my favorite dress of my sister's. It was a big disappointment. But still, I guess you could say that I lived in a kind of denial. I hoped that I wasn't that different, I hoped it didn't show, I hoped no one would notice. I didn't know if I was actually the way that everyone kept insinuating I was. I didn't want to know!

This created a lot of tension. I was in anguish basically and, after being told a few times about Jesus and heaven and how I wasn't going there, I felt awful. I got the message: *There is something wrong with me.* To combat this feeling, I tried to genuinely be what everyone wanted. I tried to put everyone else first. I tried to live up to everyone else's expectations. But that was exhausting and ultimately seemed impossible. So eventually I switched to a different tactic: I tried my best to *pretend* to be like everyone else. I memorized Bible verses and stories and learned all there was to learn about how to be a good Christian. I tried to embody being the perfect Christian according to my small country Lutheran church's standards. The idea of understanding myself, or just being myself, was light-years away. I couldn't even think of the possibility that figuring out what would make me happy or free or feel at peace was important enough to risk offending or upsetting other people (or Jesus). I thought this for so long that I was very far away from knowing what would make me happy. This small church community was my whole life and it never occurred to me that facing who I was, that learning the deepest truths about who I was, was a better choice. I didn't know it at the time, but I needed to come out to myself before I could hope to come out to anyone else.

While I was pretending and deflecting, it was a lot like lip-synching at camp. I gave the performance of my life as a star Christian. I was the most Christian a Christian could be. Deep down, though, I was hoping that people wouldn't see past the fake layers all the way to the real me—which I had yet to really know about! And things were getting tougher. The tension was building. The real me was popping out all over! The knowledge—the clues—was everywhere. I couldn't *not* float like a Disney princess through Vacation Bible School, always up on the balls of my feet. So I kept tying the Bible to me as a way to weigh me down. Jesus and religion supposedly gave me hefty heft. God gave me weight . . . and eventually depression.

I was so young, but I discovered a deep truth about myself: I *am* different. And what makes me different is so deeply a part of who I am that it was unlikely to be prayed away. I discovered that who I am was unlikely to change. I still felt wrong somehow, but my perspective changed to include at least the possibility that I could be me and be okay. What a gift it was, just when I needed it. I wish I could say that this discovery came to me because of my willingness, because of my intelligence, to see that coming to terms with this would make me happier. Nope. This epiphany was forced on me. The tension had become so great—I had suffered and hid and covered up so much—that something had to give. I'm grateful that what gave was my resistance to just looking squarely at who I am.

You can do the same. That's the lesson if there is one: epiphanies will make you happier. Yes, this particular self-realization wasn't exactly my choice. But I've learned my lesson. Today I welcome this kind of self-discovery. I welcome any chance to see a little deeper into what it means to be human. The more I see about myself, the more I see about everyone. I love bringing that to the world so much that I'm willing to keep looking and learning. You can be willing too.

YOUR FAVORITE

List your favorite things. There are two parts to this exercise: enjoy listing your favorites and also enjoy how you list them. Where do you look for an answer about your favorites? What makes something a favorite? Do you see any patterns or overall clues about you in your list? Are there clues about what you enjoy or what kinds of things attract you?

What is your favorite

ice cream flavor? _____

insect? _____

movie?_____

song?_____

subject to learn about? _____

toenail polish color? _____

president?_____

THINGS

game? _____

fish? _____

breakfast cereal? _____

book or play? _____

thing to do on Saturdays? _____

time to take a bath? _____

sport? _____

kind of math problem? _____

season? _____

singer? _____

color to wear? _____

food? _____

4

. . .

HAVE YOUR EMOTIONS

Why do we have emotions?

All *why* questions like this tend to be dead ends because they are mostly impossible to answer. A much better question is, "How can I improve my relationship with my emotions?" or, "How can I learn to welcome my emotions?" Sure, with luck, you might eventually find your way toward understanding more about emotions, but big questions like "Why do I feel?" are, at best, frustratingly hard explorations. At worst, they create utterly insufferable, endless mental debates that keep you believing you might be doing something wrong. You could be spending that time practicing being open to whatever is going on in your emotions. Also, because this particular *why* question is so hard to answer, you might even start to believe that having feelings is wrong. And that's a very dangerous notion. Emotions can't be wrong. How you treat your emotions, and how you treat yourself when a strong emotion arises, can lead you toward or away from freedom, but that has nothing to do with feelings being right or wrong.

Perhaps, just perhaps, implied in the question "Why do I have emotions?" is the desire to get rid of them. You might hope that if you can answer the *why* of your feelings, you will be able to change them, or prevent them somehow. You can't do either of those things.

Have you ever stopped to ask a different *kind* of question entirely, like, "What's so bad about emotions?" or, "Why are people so hung up about being sad or angry or depressed?" If you are really going to embrace and accept yourself, you need to be willing to feel lots of things. You need to challenge (or at least begin to question) the very fundamental things you've been taught about how and what you are allowed to feel. You need to question the idea that some emotions are okay to express and some are not okay. You need to question what it means about you if you "fly off the handle" or "can't stop crying" or "can't get over" something. Often the emotion itself isn't the problem, the way you react to it is. Often the emotions themselves don't cause a lot of suffering. It's what you think certain emotions *mean* that gets you, and gets to you.

Having emotions can feel like a weakness, which is why many of us try to wall ourselves off from them. You get the idea (somehow) that there is a certain, perhaps safe range of feeling, and that if you dip below that range or even climb too high above it, you are in danger. You were taught that in order to be an acceptable kid (and then an acceptable adult) you needed to stay within the safe emotional zone. Fall below the safe zone into depression and it's all your fault—how could you let it happen again? Skyrocket above into total unabashed joy and you're crazy and out of touch with reality. But, of course, feeling bad about leaving the safe zone doesn't keep us from leaving the safe zone. Here's a secret: *You were born to be outside the safe zone.* You were born to be all over the emotional map. You're human, and emotional self-policing is not possible. To try to have only "acceptable" emotions in only "acceptable" amounts is craziness. (Maybe something like this makes us feel crazy *because* it is impossible.) Trying to force yourself into a narrow range of acceptable feelings is useless and frustrating because it can't be done. Am I the only one who's noticed this? Spending oodles and oodles of time trying to keep yourself from really feeling too low or too high or too unsafe or too angry or too ecstatic takes so much *effort*, is so impossible, that of course you end up feeling totally inadequate to the task. And just as a tiny reminder, *you are inadequate to the task* if the task is taking your sentient-feeling-human emotions and suppressing them out of existence. Also crazy is the idea that you can feel only the emotions you like and never feel the ones you don't like. Humans feel all over the place, and you can't rein in emotion. Why even try?

Before we go any further, I want to break something down for you. I might be oversimplifying here, but there is a very important question we need to discuss. *What is an emotion?* It seems so basic, so simple, that maybe you've never thought about it. An emotion has two basic parts. An emotion is energy in your physical body with a word attached to it. That's it. Now, for you there might also be a lot of *meaning* attached to the word for the emotion, but that's actually a different and unnecessary step. It goes like this: You feel a constriction in your chest like it's a whole lot heavier than the rest of your body. The feeling is familiar; your brain knows the word for this: *sadness.* Then come the interpretations. Whether an emotion is acceptable, whether you should feel it, how it makes you weak to have it, how you might not survive if you fully feel it—all of that gets added later. And it's all actually not an intrinsic part of any emotion. If you take a chance and spend some time with what you're feeling, you have the opportunity to divorce the actual body sensations from *what you think they mean*. Part of the key to that is learning to accept and cultivating a willingness to explore the sensations of whatever emotion is occurring.

Sometimes we try to clamp down on an emotion as a way of dealing with what we think it means. For example, your boss or teacher says something that ticks you off to no end. It might be a criticism about how you're performing, or some comment about something in the news that just rubs you the wrong way. For the purpose of this example, let's say you're really angry. So angry, in fact, that you feel like you could really let your boss have it, that you could really tear into them with what you think of them and how they should be and how they shouldn't talk to you like that and on and on. Whatever the basics of anger are, whatever the actual feelings in the chest or throat or belly are, they have now gotten interpreted as "They're wrong, they're bad, I've got to do something about this." Now, let's say at this point you also get concerned. If you snap at or blow up at your boss, you might lose your job. Or if this is at school and it's a teacher, you might get detention or worse. You realize that "They're wrong, they're bad, I've got to do something about this" is going to get you into trouble. And so you clamp down, you keep your mouth shut.

Let me be clear: the wisdom to recognize that it may not be wise to yell at your boss is a good thing. What is going on internally needs your attention, though. Yes, don't yell at your boss. But you must honor and express the anger somehow. Being angry with someone (and remember, I'm just picking one emotion as an example) can feel good. You can scream by yourself in your house and let off steam and be done with it. You could just express it and move on. But here's what usually happens. A strong emotion like anger tends to stick around longer than the incident that provoked it, especially if it goes unexpressed. You tend to intellectualize. You have imaginary conversations in your head with the person you feel the anger toward. The incident might stick with you for the rest of the day or week or you might stay angry and resentful for a year! You might feel the need to justify (inside or outside your head) why you still feel angry, spinning fake interactions and coming up with reasons why the person you're angry with deserves it.

But, of course, you don't need to justify how you feel. You need to express how you feel. Because emotions don't have to mean anything, your feeling them doesn't have to mean anything either. Actually, the only way out of something like anger is through it, but in an appropriate way. And if you go through it with consciousness, it's less likely to linger. With something like anger, if people aren't able to express it, they often get stuck just holding on to the energy of it, just carrying it around forever, and ultimately that's not helpful.

So how can you consciously express anger? Why should you even try to release it? When anger (or whatever unacceptable hot-button emotion is tough for you) can be fully expressed in a safe way, you will see immediately that it's *okay*. You didn't explode, you didn't "lose yourself," or whatever. You finally felt the strong emotion that was frightening you, and *it didn't last forever*. It's only when you allow the emotion to play out its role that you are able to see how little power emotions have. It's only when you allow yourself to truly express it that you see: there's nothing dangerous or wrong or bad about feeling things. We'll talk about specific methods for expressing emotions in healthy ways a bit later. For now, know that expressing your anger *without* yelling in your boss's face is not only possible, it's freeing.

Ultimately there is a big difference between feeling an emotion and acting on it the way we think we should act on it. They are two different things, but we tend to think of them as one total package. You can be angry and not scream in your boss's face. You can be depressed and still exercise. As you work on expressing emotions in healthy ways, you can start to experiment with untangling emotion from action. The suffering is in the four-part system:

1. Sensations in the body

2. A word for those sensations (*anger*)

3. What it means ("He thinks I'm an idiot. How dare he?")

4. What we *do* because of what it means

People don't usually get that these parts don't necessarily have to go together, and so they will call all four parts lumped together an emotion; for example, parts 1 through 4 are anger. Because the four steps are seen as one step, it's often your actions that get your attention. It's not necessarily the feeling of anger that you notice; what gets your attention and gets you interested in changing your life is the consequences of yelling in your boss's face! Or with depression, you may get so tired of sitting around, of never having energy to get out and do things that you like, that you are willing to seek help and try a different approach. The behaviors that go with certain emotions can bring you the motivation to look a little deeper.

But let me remind you one more time, don't try to change your feelings. Expressing and changing are not the same thing. You can work on changing your *behavior* eventually, but you can't change your emotions. You don't want to fall for the lie that you need to feel a certain way before you can act a different way.

People often assume at least a couple of untrue things about emotions. And these false assumptions contribute to their actions around certain emotions. The assumptions go like this.

1. **Feelings are forever. You will always feel this way and you are powerless to do anything about it.** Not true. Everything is constantly changing. Right down to our atoms and strings of string theory, everything is changing all the time. And you experience this with emotions, right? At 3:00 you feel elated, you are on top of the world, and by 4:00 you feel like *garbage,* as the French might say. Sometimes that shift can happen in thirty seconds! You can't make emotions last or disappear. And it means nothing about you that you can't.

2. **If you feel a certain way, you need to act a certain way.** Here is that idea of untying behavior from physical feelings in the body again. People think, *If I am depressed, then I should be sitting around and slumping and feeling bad.* Here's an interesting take on things: What would happen if you felt depressed and went for a long walk in the woods? What would happen if you felt angry and released the energy by laughing really loud? I'm not saying you *should* do these things, only that they are possible. You don't need to feel trapped into certain behaviors because of certain emotions.

3. **Your feelings are your own fault.** This is the worst lie! If this is an issue for you, you tend to assume that the way you feel means something about who you are and what you deserve, and how "weak" you are that you can't just "get over it." That's all baloney! And while we are on the subject, it may be technically true that you can change your behavior around emotions. But this takes time, and it has nothing to do with stopping yourself from feeling your emotions altogether. And if you can abandon the idea that emotions are your fault, you will have the guts and patience to do this.

Because of the three assumptions listed here, people tend to shove aside their intense feelings instead of truly experiencing their emotions. This is quite a shame because (in general) emotions cannot hurt you. You will not die from being angry, or shrivel up from being sad. Is it possible to simply feel whatever you feel without judgment and without trying to alter or turn off the feelings? Can you feel without an analysis about what your feelings *mean* about who you are?

You probably have a favorite emotion. I don't mean the one that feels best necessarily, I'm talking about the one that you find yourself feeling most often. Sometimes you have one or two emotional grooves that you find very comfortable. I would encourage you to be open to the idea that you can and do feel all kinds of emotions, not just the ones you might be used to. It might be helpful to "try on" something like anger if you consider yourself someone who doesn't get angry.

Feelings are not flaws. They are not weaknesses. They are a

natural part of being human. One key to expressing emotions in a healthy way is acceptance. Always acceptance. With acceptance, the approach to anything you're feeling is welcoming and exploratory; you're doing your best to accept the physical feelings in your body, accept that you might have opinions or thoughts about your emotions, accept that you are trying and this is a new process for you. When in doubt, come back to acceptance, to yes: Yes, you're human. Yes, you feel. Yes, maybe you don't want to feel. Yes, it will pass. Yes, it's scary. Yes, it's hard. Whatever it is, it will be improved by accepting what's happening and paying very close attention. How do you learn to accept? With time. With patience. With a willingness to stay open to new information.

Start a practice of a daily joy list.

List anything that brings you joy. Keep the list in your phone or by your bed. Add three items when you wake up each morning. About once a week, read over your list and don't try to prevent your emotions from rising up and out of your personal safe zone as you read. After three weeks, look to see how keeping track has changed your outlook.

#DearJeffrey

I'm scared. I don't know what will happen if I just feel things. I don't like being out of control. What if something bad happens?

Well, I don't know the future. I have a few guesses, but I actually have no clue what will happen when you, specifically, start to feel emotions you are used to avoiding. There are a couple of points about fear that might be helpful to keep in mind as you explore your emotions.

Fear is your best indication that you are headed in the right direction. When something threatens your status quo, when something looks like it might promise a big change, it will come with fear. Fear is a natural instinct and there is nothing wrong with it per se. But the proportion of fear is usually way out of whack.

Fear assumes your inadequacy. Fear makes it all about you and whether you can handle the life you're living. Emotions are happening in your body. Emotions are happening in your life. Usually they are here to help you understand how you and your world work. I'm thirty-eight years old as I write this and I have faced many fears that seemed huge at the time and turned out to be almost nothing. In fact, my fears were actually a chance for me to grow. On the rare occasions when what fear promised me would happen actually did happen, I got the chance to see that the thing I feared did not break me. Whatever the horrible, monstrous thing was that I was supposed to be afraid of turned out to be almost nothing.

Everyone has their own definition of *bad things that might happen to me*, but a life of trying to avoid certain feelings and being deathly afraid of what you might feel sounds pretty bad already. In other words, there is very little that could happen to you that would be worse than living with fear. So what have you got to lose by working with your fear?

When you give yourself space and permission *to feel* an emotion, something wonderful might happen. You might open up; you might change your life for the lovelier. Who knows? Don't stay suffering and avoiding interacting with your feelings because you think avoiding feelings keeps you safe. You can practice being brave, little by little. You can take tiny steps and congratulate yourself for trying new things.

You can look at the unknown future as a fearful, awful prospect, or you can see it as *exciting*. Don't worry about getting it wrong. Just go slowly, and try feeling the things you usually avoid.

I'm scared of the way I feel sometimes, like it might be too much. If I give over to my feelings, won't I get lost in them?

The reason you know you can handle anything that happens to you emotionally is because you've handled everything so far. It's a great indication of your strength that you have faced a million things that you thought would be too much for you, and they turned out to be just fine. You turned out to be just fine. What I'm trying to point out is that this might be a pattern for you: There is something you think you can't handle. You decide to try it or you're forced by circumstances to try it. You find out that it wasn't that big of a deal.

How many times do you need to go through that before you begin to suspect that there isn't much in this world that you can't handle? Fear is so often in hyperdrive, exaggerating everything into a life-or-death struggle. I do know that actual tragic, horrible things happen. I know some things really seem unsurvivable. But you have always survived so far. This is important to remember because what we are talking about are sensations in your body and your reactions to them. Believe me, you are strong enough to face that. And you are strong enough to make decisions about whatever happens after you start to experiment with your emotions. By the way, you might even like what happens after! When you allow yourself to accept your emotions, even if they are "negative," you almost always also feel relief. If, for instance, you grant yourself the permission to just be sad, then while you experience the sadness, you will also be free of the burden of trying to pretend you aren't sad. And let's not forget, eventually the sadness will pass.

Some people can just get over emotions, or they don't seem to have them. Why can't I be like that?

We're not talking about *some people* in this book. Read the cover! We're talking about *you*. Yes, some people's feelings may seem to hide a bit further from the surface, but that's not necessarily a good thing, nor does it mean they don't feel anything at all. And notice I said *seem* to hide. . . . You don't actually know what someone else's emotional life is like behind the face they decide to show the world. Even if it were true that some people could "get over" their emotions, would someone who doesn't express emotions as dramatically or in the same way you do automatically have a better, happier life? Who knows? I don't know. I *do* know that ultimately you've got the emotions you've got. I've got the emotions I've got. We get to work with them. We get to embrace and accept them. (This is why accepting your emotions is ultimately the same as accepting yourself.) Comparing your relationship to certain emotions to what you think is someone else's relationship to their emotions is a waste of time because you just don't know what's going on for them. There's no reason to be jealous of someone you can't be sure even has what you want.

Bottom line: You don't know what someone else does when they get home or when they're alone. You don't know what someone else feels in private, and you don't know whether they're actually happy. The things people are willing to show in public are so often different from their private experiences. We all tend to filter what we show others. So comparing your own unfiltered raw emotional experiences with someone else's curated and specifically modulated emotions isn't fair. It's not fair to *you* when you compare yourself with others, and it's not fair to *them*. We all have emotions. We all can find them difficult from time to time. If you start with the assumption that we are alike deep down, that we all go through hard times and glorious times—that we all feel things deeply—you start with a connection instead of a comparison. Doesn't that seem like a nicer way to relate to people?

By the way, I have never encountered anybody who didn't express emotions in some way, or who could "get over" emotions in any way at all. And actually, as far as I can tell, most people struggle with accepting the whole of their emotional responses throughout their lives. That's why I wrote a whole chapter about it! For example, the idea that it's possible to—and that you should—suppress certain emotions is a misconception that a lot of people believe. Some people grow up being told that they mustn't have emotions, or at least they mustn't show them. But of course we all feel emotions anyway. This sometimes results in parents trying to pass the same rules of emotional suppression they learned on to their kids. What everyone needs more of are parents and heroines and teachers who are willing to express emotions at healthy times and in appropriate ways as a model for others.

> Maybe what I'm feeling is fine.
> But I'm not sure of the difference between
> an appropriate response to what I'm
> feeling and the wrong thing to do.
> What if I make a mistake?

When we are allowed to fully and safely explore and feel our feelings, we can see clearly what to do next. It's when we think anger is a *problem* and we assume that we shouldn't be feeling it or that we should control it that we end up acting out in a way that puts our job or relationships at risk. What we get when we allow ourselves to feel is space; we get time. So in that way, you can't make a mistake. It's not a right or wrong thing. It's about acceptance.

Let's say some emotion is coming up for you at work or school; it could be anything from depression to anger to joy. You really feel it in your body. You might need to find an excuse to go somewhere private and experiment with it. This is what bathrooms are for (well, besides the obvious). You can get a hall pass or excuse yourself from that meeting and cry or jump up and down in a stall for two minutes. The sneak-out-and-feel plan is available to most of us. If you experiment with this, if you give yourself a break from the situation where you are experiencing a difficult emotion and allow yourself to have a reaction—any reaction—you have taken a step toward freeing yourself from suppressing your feelings.

But I know not every situation is perfect. If you *just can't* excuse yourself to go somewhere (semi)private, then you might need to do your best and ride things out until you can sneak away somewhere.

No matter what, you must give yourself the chance to feel *at some point*. Maybe nothing will "come out," maybe it will feel like the moment has passed, or maybe you will be able to have a great relief from finally being able to just let 'er rip and pour out what's been going on for you. (More on this later.)

Again, the bottom line is to practice not judging or criticizing or even analyzing what happens. Just let yourself express whatever is in you the best way you know how, and once you've had that release, your mind will be more focused and able to contemplate the situation more clearly.

How to Practice Expressing Emotions (in Case Nobody Told You)

Phrases like "just feel your feelings" and "embrace your emotions" are tricky because without a lot of context in terms of *your own experiments and experiences* with emotions, the words may not mean much to you. Let's talk a bit more deeply about the steps in approaching and accepting how you feel. If you want to be proactive, if you sense that there is a lot of freedom waiting for you when you learn to accept your emotional responses, then here's how to get started!

1. Pick a time and place to practice and explore.

Sometimes all a strong emotion needs is an open door. It seems entirely counterintuitive, and I'm not saying that you can "schedule" emotions. How crazy would it be to add "feel really depressed from 3 to 4 on Tuesday" to your calendar? No. That's not how it works.

But you can schedule a time to feel *whatever* you are feeling at that given moment. Often you have some inkling, some vague sense, of something going on emotionally and you think it could be helpful to give yourself time to explore it. This is more like "I give myself permission to feel whatever is there to feel for half an hour after work for a week." The point is that you have a time where you won't be suppressing or pushing down or trying to control.

Also counterintuitively, if there is an emotion that seems overwhelming, you can experiment with scheduling a time to be open to that too. If you lose someone you love through death or a breakup, you need to grieve. But there is such a thing as getting totally caught up in the grief—even weeks or years later—and letting the grief rule your life. There are certain emotions that can be so strong (and you try to avoid them so much) that they spontaneously come up and take over when you're at work or at the supermarket. If it seems like your life has been taken over by a strong emotion like grief to the extent that you find it hard to function, you can experiment with scheduling a time to familiarize yourself with grief. Often an emotion simply wants to be acknowledged and accepted (just like us!), and this is a way to make sure that there is a chance it will happen. In this example, you could set a clear time with a beginning and an end during which grief is accepted and celebrated and maybe felt, but definitely given permission to be there. Again, it's not about turning emotions on and off, which isn't possible. It's about choosing a time where an emotion will be welcome if it's there. When the time is up, you can say, "Thank you, grief," and give yourself permission to dry your eyes and promise yourself that you'll come back to that safe emotional space at a later time. The end of the allotted time is not necessarily about moving on or having any specific goal; the whole process is about giving that strong emotion a window of time where it is accepted and allowed and center staged, so that it is less likely to try to take center stage in situations where that doesn't take care of you.

Start small, maybe about fifteen minutes or a half hour. Set the timer on your phone.

2. Let your feelings out.

This may seem obvious by now, but don't hold back. Try to be as welcoming as you can toward the emotions you might experience. Once you have picked a time to explore (or even if the time has picked you), do your best to remain as open as possible to the experience. An emotion is like a visitor, and you can do a lot to make that visitor feel welcome. As we've discussed, a huge part of any emotion is the physical sensations in the body, and some emotions beg you to physicalize them. Anger has a lot of energy behind it, so perhaps you find a safe way to use up a lot of energy. Choose something like hitting a pillow or screaming or running for a short time (or a long time if you're really ticked off). The point is that there is often a physical way to engage an emotion. When you energetically "dance with" what you're feeling, it literally moves around as you move around. And the added bonus here is that it is an automatic sign to you and the emotion that there is nothing wrong. Anger gets dangerous when we clamp it down and try to control it or pretend it isn't happening, not when we release the anger by running around the block sixteen times.

There are emotions that feel like an opposite energy to anger, of course. They seem to move inward more than they try to get out. I find it really helpful to sit on the floor sometimes or go into a small private space like a closet (I'm serious!) to take a moment and honor a feeling. This is where scheduling a time to explore helps because, as we've discussed, you can't always do this when an emotion comes on suddenly at work or school. But when you have privacy, it works wonders. (And remember that tip from earlier: bathroom stalls when no one else is around are a great place for this type of thing.)

You don't need to experience some kind of healing epiphany or cry every time you take a moment with your emotions. But even if it's just for a short time, giving up needing to control yourself and just sighing or crying or screaming or breathing can be a beautiful thing. There is the possibility that nothing at all will happen. That's okay too. But perhaps within the safe, private space you've set up (if you can find one), you'll finally get to experiment with expressing something that you thought was wrong or bad or somehow inexpressible. When you express an emotion, you honor it, and you also honor yourself. And remember, you don't need to get it "right." There is no right. You can stumble and be unsure and feel weird about it. You might not even feel the emotion you expected. You might in fact feel immense resistance to even trying something like this. But that's okay. You still get credit for considering it.

3. Congratulate yourself.

This is perhaps the most important bit. Making yourself vulnerable is not easy! Most of us have been shamed in regard to our feelings for so long that it takes great courage to go against our instincts. You deserve positive reinforcement. So it's essential to take a moment when you're done to acknowledge what a rip-roaring accomplishment it is just to be willing to *try*. And take note: I didn't say it was a big accomplishment to feel better or end up smiling. The result is not the important part! Be glad for, and willing to celebrate, your bravery in trying.

Hero/ine

Ali Forney was emotional and passionate and unafraid to live boldly. When Ali was thirteen, he was kicked out of his home and forced to live on the streets of New York City because of his sexuality. Instead of disappearing or giving up, and instead of living in fear about how he felt, Ali became a vocal advocate for other LGBT people who were homeless like him. Instead of staying stuck and fearful around his emotions and what had happened to him, he decided to help other people. Ali worked to educate other young people he met about HIV prevention and safe sex. This was in the early 1990s, and people who had been abandoned by their families and forced to live on the streets needed a friend. They needed someone who had felt what they were feeling and had survived.

When a few of the LGBT people he knew from the street went missing or were murdered, he tirelessly advocated that the NYPD investigate, until, when he was twenty-two years old, Ali himself was found murdered.

Today there is a safe place in New York City for LGBT homeless youth to go when they need help. This place provides various forms of support and counseling so that the people it helps can accept themselves and how they feel and begin to rebuild their lives. The Ali Forney Center honors Ali's vibrant spirit by reaching out to people like Ali who need a supportive place to stay.

RISKING SADNESS

When I was a kid, I felt like I wasn't allowed to be sad. Of course I did feel sad sometimes anyway, but it was like I wasn't allowed to express it or tell anyone. What the people around me thought of as "boy" emotions were okay; I could get angry, or even aggressive, and that was fine. But somewhere I got the idea that sadness and empathy were off-limits.

Then a few years ago I suddenly became aware of this buildup of sadness. It was like all the times I didn't feel like I was allowed to be sad as a kid had finally combined and were beating on the dam of my emotional control system. I don't know anything about past lives, but it even felt like the sadness was bigger than my own history. It felt overwhelming. And even though it seemed scary, I knew it was time to feel it. I needed to embrace the sadness, to go *through* it, in order to stop being afraid of it.

I committed to being sad. I told myself that I would feel it all, I would take the risk, I would cry, I would have whatever reaction I was going to have, and I would see how it went. And guess what happened. Not much. I cried. I walked around sad for a few days. I mourned the things that were sad and had always been sad. I grieved. I let it out and it wasn't overwhelming after all. It wasn't even all that interesting. Except, of course, that I felt a million times better once it was okay to be sad. And yes, sadness still comes and I'm so glad I have a different relationship with it. It isn't scary. It's clear that it won't last forever. And now sadness is even nice when it comes around: it can feel good to be able to express it.

5

...

LET GO OF PUNISHMENT AND CONTROL

Do you ever feel like life is punishing you? Do you ever feel like so many bad things are happening to you that it must be personal? *Maybe life hates me,* you think. *Maybe life is out to get me. Maybe I'm being punished for some bad thing I did or some way I am.* If you've ever felt like that, you're not alone!

Actually, most of us feel that way from time to time. And, conversely, if everything is going right and you think you are doing everything right and something wonderful happens, you can feel like life has finally recognized that you're special and is *rewarding* you. What I want to point out in this chapter is how that idea, that life punishes or rewards you, really isn't helpful. The idea of punishment and reward, and what it suggests about controlling life, is something we all need to let go of. I want to help you give up the control you think you're supposed to have over something as wild and wonderful and surprising as life itself. Not only is "life's rewarding you" or "life's punishing you" a false, layered-on view of how things work, it makes

everything in life about you and *about your worth*. The sooner you
can let go of the notion that life is all about how you're performing,
the better you'll feel. The sooner you let go of the idea that you can
control how life goes, the better you'll feel. When everything is about
you and you think you should be in control, you miss some pretty
awesome stuff that doesn't fit into the story of your personal punishment and reward. Actually, you miss out on most of life.

It makes perfect sense that when your boyfriend breaks up with
you, you feel like you're being punished, and when you get that pro-
motion at work, you might feel like it's a reward somehow. You were
likely given that as the only context for life events when you were
little. To whatever extent, as you grew up, your parents (or whoever
raised you) were your whole world. Early on, depending on how
things went for you, you didn't even see or meet that many people
outside your family. So much of your early environment was about
how your family treated you. And for so many of us, how our family
treats us is all about punishment versus reward. Do what your
parents want and get a cookie, do what they don't want and get sent
to your room. Whatever it looked like in your house growing up, life
was likely about trying to avoid punishment and seek rewards.

Once you've become used to that system, how can you let go of
punishment and reward? How can you choose something else now
that you aren't that tiny kid anymore? You can attempt to see life as
it is. You can attempt to see life as big as it is. Life is a huge mystery.
The planets don't care how you did on your algebra test. And there
is a reason for that: the universe is a vast place and you are not the
only thing in it. So one thing you can do right away is keep in mind
the biggest possible perspective as you make decisions and live your
life. With all these planets and stars and rivers and mountains, it
would be odd if all of it were centered on whether you're passing or

failing. It would be strange if all this grandeur and splendor were dependent on how you said the wrong thing to a friend. It can't be. It isn't. This world and this universe is about so much more, and if you can remember that—if you can focus on that—you'll be ready to fully live.

When you're a kid, you have no autonomy. You aren't at a point where it's even possible to try to say, "You know what, family? You wanna control my life based on whether I do what you say? I'm going to live somewhere else." As crazy as it is to imagine a two-year-old leaving her parents and striking out on her own, it's just as crazy to be a teenager or even an adult still living under the two-year-old's system of right/wrong, good/bad, I'm being punished / I need to work for rewards. We're lucky there are ways out of that little kid's system.

What's another way out? How else can you let go of punishment and reward? By being present. Punishment and reward are actually tied to the past. Supposedly, you're being punished or rewarded for something you did in the past, but the past is actually an illusion. It's not happening here and now. It's a memory. It doesn't actually exist. When you feel like life is punishing you, try listening to birds or noticing the colors around you. Try to focus on something that's happening now—right now. Birds never sing about what happened yesterday because they know how to fully live this moment without dragging what they did then into the picture. Any idea of punishment reaches back into a (maybe not accurately remembered) past, then interprets what we remember, then assigns blame for it (to you), and then gets you feeling bad in the present. But often there is nothing in your *present* to feel bad about. You can't change the past and you shouldn't spend your present trying to do so. Being here and seeing the present clearly is your best shot at having the life you want—a life free of taking everything personally.

And to be clear about punishment: it doesn't work very well. You know this is true inside yourself. Withholding affection from yourself or punishing yourself isn't a very effective way to change your own behavior. People who feel left out, like they are being singled out, like they are being abused by life, aren't too enthusiastic about changing. How many times does it take to punish a kid before they get it? And what do they get? If you're trying to teach a kid that cake for breakfast isn't very good for their health, will punishing them when they want cake really teach them anything? If a parent chooses to punish a kid, especially without talking about why, the parent runs the risk of sending a bad message. Instead of learning that cake isn't the best choice at the start of the day, a kid might "learn" that *they are bad for wanting cake* and that they deserve to be punished for liking cake. This child might even take that idea (what is happening is happening because I'm bad) out of childhood and into adult life.

So how can you drop those ideas? How else can you let go of punishment and reward? By giving yourself love. Love is the antidote to taking things personally and trying to control. Contrary to what you might have heard, it's fairly easy to love yourself. Most of us started out in this world pretty fresh and pretty loving toward ourselves. You must reconnect with that. You must be kind to yourself. Let yourself off the hook. Keep in mind your best qualities. Ask someone who loves you what they like most about you. Put those things in a note. Read the note every morning. Go on walks with yourself. Start to see yourself from the outside. How would you treat a friend who was struggling with feeling punished all the time? You would treat them with love. You deserve that acceptance and love too.

One more note here: as I said before, most people assume that life is punishing them *because of who they are.* You might think, *Life is doing this to me for a reason. It must be because I'm bad.* That's a natural, even logical, thing to think! And, yes, the flip of that is thinking that you are rewarded for who you are too. You get good rewards because you (finally) did something right. The big, fat philosophical question in all of this: what if you are already and without a doubt a good person, regardless of what happens to you in life? The things that happen to you have very little to do with who you are *as a person.* Things don't happen because of who you are. You lose your wallet or win the lottery not because of anything you *are.* If you can divorce your *ownership* of the things that happen in your life from the things themselves, you can end up having a better time. At least that's my experience of it!

Letting go of the concept of punishment versus reward is a big part of everything in this book. Do you see yourself as a person who constantly deserves the bad stuff in life—who constantly deserves to be punished? Well, you're not! When you start to see that life is not about punishment, then you won't be someone who *deserves* to be punished because no matter what happens to you, it's not a punishment. The big issue here is that if you feel like life is punishing or rewarding you, your relationship with the things that happen to you (all of life, really) is suddenly antagonistic. In that worldview, you are separate from life and you are being treated a certain way by life. But you are as much a part of life as anything else. You belong here as much as anyone else does.

Finish these sentences.

Don't try to control your answers—or say the right thing. Try to write as fast as you can without thinking too much about it.

A good mother would never . . .

_____

A family should always . . .

_____

I would be so hurt if a friend ever . . .

_____

The perfect day would always have to include . . .

_____

Go back and read over your answers. Are there any assumptions there that you could let go of? Are there any reasons for punishing yourself or other people that you see? Are there any invisible standards or shoulds that might be preventing you from being free?

#DearJeffrey

If life isn't about punishment and reward, wouldn't it be boring? If I stop thinking about life as hating me and punishing me, shouldn't I also stop thinking about life rewarding me? Don't I get any good stuff? Punishment and reward go together, don't they? I'm confused . . .

We touched on this briefly, but here's a little more of the scoop: when you are no longer spending all your time trying to decide whether everything that happens is a punishment or reward for you, you open up. When your mind is not trying to control outcomes or figure out whether life likes you, you are truly present. Letting go like this opens you up to all the possible "rewards beyond rewards" of being in the moment: You feel relieved. You feel like a part of life. You know you belong. Chances are you will even feel glad to be alive, or we could simply say you will finally start to feel alive. So, yes, you get good stuff and how! But you need to be willing to ditch the dualistic ideas of hoarding all the good stuff and pushing away all the bad stuff, and simply experience each situation as it comes.

I realize that reward is a tricky thing to think about letting go of. Punishment isn't pleasant. You see why a person would want to give that up. But reward? Reward seems so good. Can't you just feel good and feel rewarded every once in a while? Do you have to give up reward if you give up punishment? In a certain sense, yes. If reward is viewed as the *opposite* of punishment, you're still trapped in a system. You aren't present and involved in life. You are still stuck in the mind-set that the things that are happening mean something about who you are as a person. I'm not saying to stop enjoying good things in life. Heavens, no. But can you enjoy them without deciding how they relate to your personal worth?

There are three steps to punishment: You believe that punishment is possible. You interpret what's happening as a punishment. You think you deserve to be punished—that you did something wrong. In this system, it makes sense that you would want to then *prove* you aren't an awful person who needs to be punished. So you might look for rewards; you might seek out some way to "make up for" the punishment you're getting at the expense of other people. Punishment and reward work so well together, so hand in hand, that we never even notice that the whole thing is based on the idea that what happens to us *means something about us.* We believe that what happens in our lives is a result of whether we are good or bad, deserving of a reprimand or an accolade. But that's 100 percent bogus. The concept of our worth being up for debate at all is total bunk.

Do bad things happen to very good people? Well, yes, clearly. Does this mean that life isn't fair? Well, as far as I can tell life is equally unfair to everybody, which makes it kind of . . . fair. Will you experience being sick? Yes. Will you experience someone you like saying something insensitive about you? Yup. Will you experience a loved one dying or a really tough breakup? Probably. And when you stop looking at these events as meaning something about you, you can clearly see that everybody else goes through all the "punishments" and "rewards" too, even people you know don't deserve punishments or rewards. Therefore, keep in mind that *you* don't deserve any of it either. It's not about you.

And, of course, we have a choice about how we see things. That's the point! Just because you don't like something doesn't mean it's a punishment. And liking something doesn't make it a reward. Sometimes things just happen to people. Dividing the people and things up into good and bad and punishment and reward arbitrarily and according to our whims is a way we try to box up life. It's a way we try to control life. But it doesn't work. Life doesn't seem to care about our whims, in the best way possible!

I'm going to say this next bit as gently as I can. This is the tough love, mama bird portion of the book, so brace yourself.

Reducing the vast, beautiful, mysterious happenings of the universe all the way down to being about what you want or don't want is incredibly selfish. It is an utterly self-centered act. Beyond there being other people on this planet who might think differently about the same events, there are trees and squirrels and comets flying by that, as we might all guess, have just as much of a right to be here as you do. You can't make it all about your desire to be validated by rewards or made penitent by punishments. You can't make it all about you, because it so clearly isn't. There's a whole world out there that you could help or participate in or just appreciate if you would let go of this idea that it all revolves around your interpretations and perspectives. The world is bigger than that. Much bigger. And to be totally honest, you are bigger than that. It's time you owned up to it. End of rant.

"It's not about you" is actually excellent news. I found that when I let go of this idea, when I stopped trying to make life happen and force my will onto life, things got really fun for me. I started to have the best time. When you're constantly comparing what *did* happen with an imaginary list of what you *wanted* to happen, you miss out on all the awesome things you didn't even know *could* happen. This is especially true if you tend to think of yourself as undeserving.

Letting go of thinking about things in terms of punishment and reward will help you see more possibilities about what you actually do "deserve." And hopefully, you will even see that life is not about deserving. You can just begin to accept and embrace whatever happens without trying to place blame or accept credit for it.

When I think about credit and blame and control and transitioning away from making life all about me, I think of growing up. It takes a lot of maturity to let these things go. It takes a commitment to another way of doing things. But before any of that, it takes an admission that you are not all-knowing; you don't have it all together. You are not perfect or 100 percent wise or even able to keep your shniz together a lot of the time. And that's okay, because that makes you human. It can be tough to admit that you are just like everyone else. You see, when you're struggling and trying hard and not getting it, and feel like you're being punished by life, and trying to control things that you can't, at least you know where you stand. It's crummy. It stinks. But it's *familiar*. You know you're struggling and you have done it for so long that it feels right somehow.

To make a commitment and say that you aren't going to struggle anymore, to say that you give up and you know you can't control things so you won't even bother . . . Whew! That takes guts because then life is almost all unfamiliar territory. What will happen? Will things fall apart? Will you fall apart? It will be like you don't know who you are anymore if you give up that fight for control. And giving up control will be wonderful.

This is where the growing up comes in. It takes maturity to stop trying to control life. Being given rewards for good behavior and punishments for bad behavior is a childish notion. That world is a kid's world and it takes some growing up to refuse to participate in the system anymore. The good news is I think you're ready to move on.

ROLLING TO A REWARD

When I look back at my days on the stage (in show after show) at York Little Theater, I have all these fond memories. All of the awkwardness I experienced at home and at church melted off my shoulders when I went through the creaky stage door in the theater's back parking lot. At the theater, I was free. I was seen. Sure, I couldn't be 100 percent out or honest. York was a small, gossipy town. But at least, if only through the guise of playing a character, my voice could be heard.

A production of *The Velveteen Rabbit* was my big breakout from the chorus and into speaking roles—speaking roles! Lines and a character arc and . . . attention! I had the role of Toy Boat. My look was fantastic: the cutest sailor cap, a huge plywood boat strapped around my shoulders, and two little roller skates poking out the bottom. I was excited. All eyes would be on me; I'd be the only one rolling past the audience, after all. Each night from backstage, about three quarters of the way through the show, I would stand stage left to hear my favorite scene. It's about the toys becoming real.

SKIN HORSE: Real isn't how you are made. It's a thing that happens to you. When a child loves you for a long, long time, not just to play with, but REALLY loves you, then you become Real.

VELVETEEN RABBIT: Does it hurt?

SKIN HORSE: Sometimes. When you are Real you don't mind being hurt.

The play is the story of a (velveteen) toy coming to realize that self-worth can be found in becoming real—about how when we're real, we don't take personally the bad things that can sometimes happen in life. It is about whether the people who play with toys understand how toys feel, whether toys are being rewarded when people play with them and punished when kid owners grow tired of paying attention to them. I learned a lot from the show. I learned how to treat myself. I learned about how to let go of how other people and life were treating me.

One night on the way to the show, life became about punishment and reward for me, and it taught me a hard lesson. *The Velveteen Rabbit* had been open for a week at the time. My dad would drive me down from our Pennsylvania farm into Maryland so that I could attend a Lutheran high school during the day, and then he would drive me back up to Pennsylvania to be in the show. That meant my father and I spent almost two hours on show days in the car together. We never really talked on these trips. I felt so out of place at home, so punished and misunderstood and unseen, that it made me sad and quiet. Well, sad and quiet and angry. I wouldn't be the first teenager who was mad at their father, I guess. I didn't feel real. I didn't feel like anyone was taking me seriously. And I couldn't yet get over the bitterness I felt about being someone the world didn't want me to be. It felt unfair. It felt wrong. It felt like I was being punished. And my dad represented all of the punishment, all of the misunderstanding, I was getting at school and church and home.

The York Little Theater stage was a safe place, though. People were at least paying positive attention to me. Actually, they were applauding my flamboyance. They were showing some gratitude for my existence. And that felt big—that meant the world to me. Which is why it seemed like a total tragedy when our car broke down on the highway going from school to the theater one day. The show was scheduled to start in an hour and a half, and I was expected in the dressing room an hour before curtain. I was stressed that we were stuck on the side of the highway. I was upset. Not only might I miss the performance, I would let down my friends at the theater—the only people at the time who I felt got me.

We sat by the road and waited for the tow truck, and waited, and waited. With each passing moment we were getting closer and closer to not making it to the theater at all. While my head was spinning with visions of my understudy trying on my costume (*my* costume, buddy!), Dad got an idea of how to pass the time: he offered to teach me how to walk.

I was thirteen. I was a little confused at first because, obviously, I knew how to walk by then. Dad explained, "I'll teach you how to walk so that the other kids don't make fun of you. You know, how to walk like a man." He was concerned for me. He was trying to help his child. But I couldn't see that. I felt hurt. I took it personally. I thought, *Why is this happening to me? What did I do to deserve this?*

I don't know where the words came from. I don't know where I found the strength, but I said, "No. I like how I walk." And then the tow truck showed up.

We made it to the theater just in time. The stage manager and I fumbled and fussed backstage to throw the plywood boat over my shoulders so I could roll out for my first line. My heart was racing. I was rolling and acting and acting and rolling, and the whole time, I couldn't get my dad's offer out of my head. How could someone live with me and not see that I walk the way I walk because *I'm me*? How could someone raise me and not know me?

I interpreted the whole thing as my dad wishing I had been

105

born a more conventionally gendered person. Unfortunately, I spent many more years feeling punished and betrayed and alone and misunderstood by my dad. And years later, he explained that he was always concerned about me when I was growing up. Well, concerned about both of us. Somewhere he got the idea that raising a "different" child was his fault. He tried to change me in any way he could because he was concerned about what other people would think about him as a parent, and about how we would be treated by others. He thought who I am was his punishment, and we both suffered for it.

My dad and I did a very special thing as the years passed, though: we changed. We gave up on taking all of it so personally. We gave up on seeing each other as punishments, and we started to see each other as people. I love Dad. He still sends me birthday cards with twenty-dollar checks in them. Actually, Mom probably sends the cards and signs both of their names. Either way, it's the thought that counts.

So what's the alternative to the punishment/reward system? You can practice not seeing the things that happen in your life as having anything to do with you. Maybe that's a tall order. You can at least try seeing the events of your life as not being a *reflection on you*. You can stop seeing each event as a reward (I should make this happen more often) or a punishment (I should avoid this at all cost). If life isn't divided up, if we let go of controlling what happens to us, what will we think about? What will life be about? I don't know! But it does sound exciting to find out, doesn't it?

Before this chapter ends, I want to make the connection between thinking about life in terms of reward and punishment and the illusion of control really clear. Reward and punishment thinking is an attempt to control life. You get into trouble when you think you can control life. You get into trouble when you think you *should* control life. You can't control what happens to you, and I want to share with you the five top myths about control, so that you won't ever feel the need to even try to control life. This is so important because when people contact me about anxiety and depression and a host of other things, I get this strong hunch that most of it comes from the illusion that we can and should control our lives. Once you have seen these five myths *and discarded them*, you will be in a great position to let go of control.

The Five Top Myths of Control

1. Control is possible all the time.

What is control exactly? Does it have something to do with getting what you want? Exerting your wishes and will over someone or something else? Have you ever been able to do that consistently? There might be some things we can control in life, but most things are way out of our control. When you think about big things like the universe or the earth, clearly you can't control the movements of planets or the clouds in the sky. (And if you ever imagined you could, perhaps you were feeling a bit out of control at the time.) The same holds true for small things. Can you control how people at work think about you? Can you control a friend's reaction when you give them bad news? Can you make good things happen to you and keep bad things at bay? Of course you can't. When you're totally honest with yourself, you begin to realize that you can't even control your own reactions to things. On the biggest and the smallest scale(s) the idea of controlling everything all the time is an illusion.

2. You should have control.

Once you believe that control exists, that it's something that's possible for humans to have in every situation, it is a short leap to the belief that you *should* have it. Remember, control isn't even possible in almost every situation, and yet most people believe it's the thing they must have. Most people think it's compulsory. Most people see it as a natural human pursuit. But actually the word *pursuit* implies some kind of choice, which isn't always the case. Most times we aren't conscious that we could ever choose *not* to try to control life. The reason I'm pointing out these things about control is because they are usually unconscious. Likely, you never examine if control is possible. You never examine if it really is something you should have. You just keep trying to do the impossible for some unknown, unstated reason (perhaps it isn't for an "unknown" reason, but we'll get to that).

3. You're failing if you don't have control.

The next thing you'll encounter if you look at this whole control myth scenario is the idea of what not having it means about you. It means you failed. It means you have done something wrong. It's not a big leap from thinking control is possible to thinking you should have it to thinking there's something wrong with you if you can't have it. If you can let go of the first two myths, you'll be able to let go of this one as well.

4. You can do something more or be something more in order to have control.

And so you try harder. Having control isn't working because it actually isn't possible (see number 1), but you don't know that. In fact, it seems possible; it seems like the thing you *should* have. You even believe that you're a failure if you can't have it. And still it isn't working. Listen, this is understandably frustrating. You're trying really hard and (because you don't know the "secret" that the whole sequence is a chain of lies) the only thing you can think of to do is try to control more. The only solution, it seems, is to try to control harder. No! Don't do it! When trying to control your life doesn't work, you try harder to control, and when that doesn't work, you try even harder to control, and on and on, assuming the whole time that there is something wrong with you if you can't control what happens to you. Good news! There's a way out. But we have one more point to discuss before I lay it on you.

5. Other people have control and you don't.

This is a related belief that builds on the first four. This is a tricky one because it relies on a bunch of assumptions about how other people's lives are going. When other people look like they are in control and like they have gotten what they want because of some magic info they have or some way they naturally are *that you aren't*, don't buy it. You can't compare your insides to someone else's outsides. You can't be sure that just because you want something they have, they want it too. And if you wait around long enough, you'll see something unpleasant or sad or tragic happen to them because those things happen to everyone. You have so little control over your life circumstances and you are not alone in that.

So how exactly do we let go of control and punishment once and for all? Well, each person's steps will likely be different, but I do know of one important ingredient. You will need to slow down. You will need to sidestep or ignore a lot of what you've been taught to believe. You will need to take deep breaths and find ways to pause and look deeply. Armed with your list of the top myths, you will need to keep an eye out for them. Look for times when you are trapped some-where in that list. This is where the slowing down comes in. Get off the control train. Refuse to participate. Let it go. Also, you will need to be willing not to feel like you. I know it sounds crazy, but you know who you are based on what you believe, and if you're going to change your beliefs, it will feel like you are changing yourself. But stick with it. I believe in you.

Maybe as you change you'll notice that life isn't all about you. Maybe you'll notice that life isn't up to you. Maybe you'll find some kindness you can do or some help you can offer, or maybe you'll see the solution to a big cause of suffering in your life or the world. Who knows? The point here is that if you ditch thinking of everything in terms of your being punished or rewarded (the what-am-I-getting approach to life), your possibilities are endless.

It's time for a week of letting go.

Every morning, in the spaces provided, write a different old worn-out belief about yourself that you are willing to let go of around that day's theme. Example: "Wednesday, Your Body: I will let go of the belief that the way my body looks is because I've done something wrong."

On each day, after you have written down what you are willing to let go of, cut out the box containing your word or phrase using scissors. Carry the paper with you, and at some point during the day consciously tear the paper up and throw it away. Let the belief go as you let the paper go. Repeat this exercise for as many weeks as you wish, using more paper.

Monday, Finances and Money:

Tuesday, Romance and Sex:

Wednesday, Your Body:

Thursday, Work and Jobs:

Friday, Friends:

Saturday, Family:

Sunday, Religion or Spirituality:

6

. . .

FORGET HATERS

What makes haters hate?

Haters aren't fun to talk about. I'll be perfectly honest. I have spent so many years dealing with the hate outside and inside me, and I get tired of talking about it sometimes. So, you may be thinking, why would I write a whole chapter about it? Because this book is my time machine. I'm partly writing this book to my ten-year-old self. I want to bring healing into as many lives as I can with the wisdom I wish I had back then . . . and I want to bring healing into my life! And if I can do that—bring healing into my own life and someone else's—yay! I'm telling you this to be very honest and to also let you know that I've been there when it comes to hate. I was bullied and hated every which way. Although it's not the most enjoyable topic for me these days, I have a ton of experience with it, and I hope that can help. The point of this chapter is to help you understand how hate works and ultimately identify and forget the haters in your life.

We've already discussed how you can see certain qualities in other people and then recognize them in yourself. Well, it works in a hater's life too. A bully hates something about you because it reminds them of something that they experience inside themselves. And clearly, they don't like to be reminded! It could be anything at all that triggers a bully: even something as simple as the way you talk.

But it doesn't always seem to be a quality or trait. What if a hater makes fun of your body? Say someone makes mean comments about you for being what they call too skinny. It's not that the hater is necessarily skinny too. It's that in the hater's mind, they think you are too skinny for a specific reason. They assume (without knowing the truth at all!) that you are skinny because you're too controlling or you are afraid to really eat or something. That's the part that the hater can (secretly) identify with. You remind the hater that *they* sometimes get controlling or get afraid. The hater hates those qualities in themselves and so feels compelled to hate what they assume are those qualities in you too.

In other words, nothing a hater does is personal. A hater isn't making fun of you because you deserve it. A hater is making fun of you because you happen to remind them of something about themselves that they hate. You happen to remind them of something they were taught to hate inside themselves, something they were taught to keep under control or deny is within them. They are trying to use hate to change you because (inside) they are trying to use hate to change themselves.

As I've said, this idea of a person seeing their own qualities in others works for anyone who is hated too. The person who's hated sees the hate, they know it's hate, they recognize that it's hate. We all know hate because chances are very good that we were taught to hate something within ourselves too. It would be rare indeed to find someone who hasn't been hated, and who also doesn't have their own experience of hate within themselves. There are also very few people (perhaps none) who have *never* hated someone or something themselves. This is how you know a hater when you see one: to some extent you were likely taught to be mean to yourself inside. (And sometimes people are taught to be mean to others outside.) We are all very much alike. At least we all have that going for us!

I say we have that going for us because it might be comforting for you to know that the haters and bullies of this world are just people too. I'm not excusing someone's hatred of someone else, but the chances are very good that haters are struggling like anybody else. They just take it out on other people. Probably they are trying to understand the world and how it works, just like you. As odd as it seems, you are not fundamentally better than your haters, *you are the same as them.* It might feel good to think of yourself as better than them, but it just isn't true. I know a lot of people find strength in feeling superior to the haters ("I would never do that!") and maybe, for some people, that's their best way to survive a hater's abuse. Maybe feeling better than the haters is how someone can get up in the morning and just make it through a day. I understand that. I actually did that for a long time. But, if I may, I want to report here that it doesn't work long term. It's not true that you're a superior human being who would never hate anything yourself, and so, in the long run, believing you are superior to haters is not sustainable. In a way (and don't blame the messenger on this one), when you feel superior to or separate from or better than your haters, you might become more like them, because you might end up hating your haters. Have you ever experienced that? Hating haters will get you nowhere because *anybody* who is hating is most likely struggling.

You don't need to add more hate to the world by hating haters. There are no "good" reasons for hate. There are no valid excuses or explanations.

So why would someone hate? Think of something or someone that you've hated. Close your eyes (then open them again so you can keep reading!) and recall a time when you really hated the stew out of someone. Who was it? How did it feel? Would you call it a happy time? Would you say it was a joyful moment for you? Would you say you were glad to be alive, or feeling really accepted and loved in that moment? Probably not, right? You can guess all of that is the same for any hater you meet. They are not happy. They are not fulfilled. They are not glad about how their lives are going.

Perhaps it's no comfort to know that haters are probably having a rough time. After all, they can't seem to keep their rough time to themselves. They want to share it with you! I realize it's a lot to ask for you to turn the other cheek with the realization that haters struggle. It might seem like a stretch to ask you to see things from a hater's point of view. The reason I write about this idea is because I would never want you to think that someone else's hate is your fault. I carried the weight of thinking *they hate me because I'm a wrong, bad person* for a long time. If I could do one thing with a time machine, it would be to go back and convince past me that hate is not my fault. I'm trying to give you all another (in my opinion the real) reason for other people's hatred toward you. It all comes down to what is going on for *them*, and it has nothing to do with any true real thing about you. If your father, nephew, school bully, boss, or manicurist hates you, it isn't your fault. You simply trigger something *in them*.

Here's a tiny tip: a hater probably somehow embodies the qualities they hate. For example, a hater hates feminine men because the hater is a man who has a feminine side that he was taught to hide and hate within himself. A bully feels compelled to try any and every tactic to get someone else to fall in line with their own internal hater system of hate. So this bully was taught that to display or even acknowledge his own feminine qualities is very wrong. No wonder he thinks that someone else whom he perceives as a flauntingly feminine man is wrong too. No wonder he would start to bully that person!

I suppose, although I don't want to assume, that if you are reading a book like this, you are more often the hated than someone who goes around hating people. Let's say you're reading these very words and you're a kid (or heck, even an adult) who is being hated regularly. I want you to realize that it's okay to get help with a hate problem. You can tell someone in authority, and if they don't do anything about the hate you're getting, you can tell *their boss*. I know you might not always feel strong enough to do that, or if you're an adult it might feel like you're risking your job. Or maybe you're a kid who feels so lacking in outlets for acceptance that you have no one you can tell. That's all terrible, and I know from experience what all of that feels like. But I also know from experience what it feels like to get help, to find support, to stop the harm that's being done to you.

And so as you experiment, as you look around and try to see the way hate works in your life and in the lives of people you know (or, yes, even in the lives of Internet trolls), you can trust me on a few things:

1. If you're being hated, it's not about you.

2. Hate emanates from, comes from, is born with, and lingers within the hater. As much as a hater might want to share their hate with other people, the hate says a ton about what is going on for the hater and almost nothing about anyone who is being hated.

3. Hating the hater doesn't work as a long-term strategy. Maybe it's a fine way to help you feel empowered in the short term, but it just won't work for long. When you hate your haters, you borrow the hate. You compound the hate. (Incidentally, that's the one way you can make someone else's hate about you.)

While a hater is doing whatever they are doing to you, you can work on ending your own side of the hatred. You can get out of the game, for your own mental health and for the benefit and health of the people around you. How awful would it be for you to take on a hater's hate by hating them, and then for you to spill that hate over onto the next person and see them spill it over onto the next? Sadly, it happens like that all the time. But you can break the hate chain. You can be the one who decides to stop the hate; the buck can stop with you.

I know this isn't an easy thing to do. What I'm talking about takes strength and courage and a willingness to not participate in what almost everyone else is participating in, namely, going around hating on yourself and others. It's a daunting assignment, but luckily there's no due date! Don't worry, you are up to the task. If you're reading a book like this, you can handle not participating in hate. You don't need to sell yourself short. What kind of life do you want? One filled with hate inside and out, or one filled with acceptance and kindness? What will you stand for? What will you practice?

Here is a story: A girl *loves* to run around and play sports. This girl is taught by her family that it is wrong for girls to run around and play sports. This girl is taught that sports are for boys and girls should never ever play sports. She stops playing and running around. She grows to hate the idea of girls playing sports. She hates when any girl plays like that. Then she goes to school and meets a girl who wants to try out for the football team. The football girl is good at sports and it reminds the hatergirl of what she gave up and she can't stand it. Her beliefs about girls and sports and all that her parents taught her swim through her head. She thinks she must defend what she was taught. She might call the athletic girl names or say hateful things to get the athletic girl to feel awful and conform and STOP PLAYING SPORTS. But that bully girl is wrong. What she was taught is wrong. Anybody can play sports.

#DearJeffrey

I feel like haters target me on purpose. Other people don't have to deal with all this. Why can't haters just leave me alone?

Haters do seem to target certain kinds of people. I know that's not what I'm supposed to say, but I have to be totally honest. It's true. They victimize certain people, and you could be one of those kinds of people. It may feel unfair, but it isn't, and I am happy to tell you why. Haters usually target certain kinds of *good* people. Being bullied is almost always a sign that you're doing something right, that you are actually some kind of awesome person. A bully targets people who they feel need to be kept in line. That's the point of bullying. Bully targets are usually free thinkers, they are usually innovators. People who are hated are often deeply compassionate, and usually have the best shot at feeling free to be themselves. Otherwise, they wouldn't need to be kept in line.

Bullies want you to be like them. They want *everyone* to be like them—to conform to the system they were taught is the right system for the human race to follow. They were raised to believe (or maybe came to believe) certain things that they strongly want you to believe too. It could be something simple, like a hater believing that people who like to read are nerds and they're wrong and bad somehow. Okay. But it doesn't just stop with their belief. They really want you to *know* that they believe good readers are wrong and bad. AND if you love to read and you're smart, they really want you to believe that you are wrong and bad. They feel compelled (strongly) to get you to believe that people who read a lot are wrong and bad. In fact, they *must* get you to believe like they do because if you don't believe like they do—if you don't go along with what a hater believes—the hater might realize that they believe the wrong thing. A bully who encounters someone who doesn't think like they do must do everything they can to persuade that person to conform to their beliefs. Clearly, if they just felt safe and happy and secure, a hater wouldn't care about trying to get other people to share their views. A hater will use any tactic to convince you to think like them: calling names, taunting, physical violence, social pressure. This comes right out of their own insecurity.

On a sheet of paper, **list your five top compliments**, the ones you love to hear about yourself.

On a separate sheet of paper **list the five worst things** that bullies and haters have always said about you. (These usually start with "too": too loud, too dumb, etc.)

Now take that separate piece of paper and tear it up. Tear up the negative list. Go ahead, destroy it. Burn it if it's safe, or rip it up and blow the pieces into the wind. Stomp and dance on the pieces. Say, "Bye, bye," and wave your hand. The idea is that this is your chance to have a ceremony, a funeral for the things you were told about yourself by haters when you were growing up.

When you're done with your ceremony, read over your top compliments and do something nice for yourself. Don't skip this part. Go to the movies or have a nice dinner.

We can talk all day long about what might be going on in a hater's head, or how a hater got to be the way they are, and that's nice, but what can you ACTUALLY DO if you're being bullied? What steps can you take to end it? What directions can you explore when the insults and abuse fly in your direction? Try some of these tips:

Agree with the Hater

This is an in-the-moment thing. Nothing diffuses a bully faster than "yes." A bully often craves the conflict. You're supposed to feel bad and fight and argue and scream and cry, but if you just turn to them and say, "You know, you're right," they have nowhere to go with it; they are stunned; they are powerless. For them, it's like trying to nail Jell-O to the wall! Of course, to use this tactic you don't *actually* have to agree with the hater deep down. You don't actually need to believe what they believe. In most cases I hope you don't believe what a hater might say to you!

This suggestion is about putting an end to the conversation. Don't say it in a defeated way, or even in an aggressive way. Just say, "I never thought of that. You are so right. Bye now," and walk away, head held high and hater confused.

Ditch the Hate Inside

While attempting to deal with an external bully, you can also put some effort into dealing with any internal ones. If you have beliefs or thoughts clanging around in your head that bully you, you can spend some time finding out how to stop them. If you go around thinking you're "so fat" or "too gay," you *are* being bullied from the inside out. The ways you treat yourself and think about yourself and the world are largely based on habit. And these habits started when you were really young, long before you could have ever made a decision to choose kind versus mean thoughts.

You must start where you are and get help if you need it, and work on changing the internal hate and judgment and bullying that might be going on every day. Abolishing outside hate is great and we should do everything we can to put an end to it, but any hate happening inside you should be changed, should be jettisoned, and should be stopped as well.

 ## Tell Someone

Haters survive on our silence. You are supposed to feel like being hated is your fault, like you did something wrong. If you believe this, you might feel too ashamed to talk, you might not want anyone to know that you "did the wrong thing" or were the wrong way that "caused" you to be hated. But this is all bunk! It's based on a bad idea. Bullying is not the fault of the bullied! And telling someone is the surest way to show you don't feel ashamed. It's the quickest way to show you know you deserve a life without being hated. Ironically, asking for help is the best way to show your strength.

Now I would like to offer some advice about whom to tell. For instance, it's not helpful to tell another hater. Do your best to find someone who accepts and understands you, someone you suspect will have a loving, respectful response. Often this is a friend, or if you're a kid, it could be your favorite teacher. The point is, tell someone who can really help, not someone who will continue the cycle of abuse or throw up their hands and say, "I don't know what to do!" And tell as many of these supportive people as you need to in order to achieve a change.

Help Someone Else

While you're working to end the hate in your own life, you can spend time helping other people who are being harassed as well. It seems weird to say that being hated has any positive effects, but one thing it can do for you is make you very empathetic when other people are in need. Get involved with politics. Join or start an organization to end hate. Immigration, women's rights, making schools safe for everyone with organizations like GLSEN—there are a lot of places where your voice and talents could make a big difference. When you feel frustrated by the haters in your personal life, it often feels great to make a broader difference in the world.

Do Something You Love

This is one that everyone should be doing all the time anyway. The best revenge when we're hated is to not care. Haters hate that. Wait, actually, who cares about the haters? That's what I love about this recommendation. It's not even close to being about them. Bullies love when everything is about them. Somehow negative attention is great to them. So let's really tick them off, shall we? Let's sing out because we love to sing out. Let's paint because we feel like it. Let's go play soccer and sit in the sunshine. Let's enjoy our time on this planet and practice not giving the bully a second thought.

Hero/ine

Audre Lorde was an American civil rights activist who worked to help black people in Germany gain acceptance and freedom. She had a ton of haters. She also stood up to the bullies she encountered who tried to stop her from helping others.

From 1984 to 1992, Audre spent most of her time living in Germany as part of the Afro-German women's movement. She worked to help African and black women in Germany dispel that culture's racist myths and gain social and political power. She raised her voice and encouraged others to raise theirs in protest of unfair treatment, even though she knew it would bring hate and resistance.

Because of Lorde's dedication and willingness to face hate and work to combat it, many people were inspired to speak out. Her work is linked to the founding of the Initiative of Black Germans, an organization that works for black rights in Germany to this day.

7

. . .

GET USED TO NOT KNOWING

We get drilled about what we want to be when we grow up from a very early age, and that question annoys the heck out of me. Why do we need to know our whole career at four and a half? Maybe you didn't realize it when you were a kid, but how people reacted to your answer probably taught you a lot. You got the message that you should grow up to be some right kind of way. And you were taught to know something unknowable, your future. Actually, you were taught to *pretend* to know your future, which is different. As you grew up, you might have gotten so used to pretending you knew that you eventually thought you really did know, or could know, how you or your future should be. And that's dangerous. The problem with what you were taught isn't just that you can't actually know the future, it's that the more you think you know about how you're supposed to be, the less chance you have to discover what might truly make you happy. The more you think you know about your future and yourself, the worse off you are.

In an earlier chapter, I wrote about trusting yourself—about honoring what you know to be true. It might seem like I'm now contradicting that advice. It might seem like a chapter on trusting what seems true to you and a chapter asking you to challenge what you know don't belong in the same book. But actually both things are valid and both bits of advice are useful for different things. Say you like wearing nail polish, as I do. Is that the same as knowing that nail polish is right or wrong? Or knowing that you are right or wrong for wearing it? Learning to recognize and trust your own instincts and what you love is a useful, wonderful experience, and it is not the same as knowing how people (especially you!) *should* be.

You get into trouble when you think you know who you're supposed to be because once you "know," you stop exploring, you stop examining. You check out . . . *from your life.* To really discover your truth, to really get to know yourself, you need to admit how little you know now about the world and yourself and how everything works. And you might have to come to terms with *not knowing.* Or at least get as comfortable as you can with "I don't know" as an answer, especially as it regards your future and who you "should be" as a person. There are a lot of questions in life, and the flip side to fear of the unknown is the freedom that comes from realizing you don't need answers. Maybe you will never find your "true self," at least not in the way you've been taught you should. And that could be the best thing that ever happens to you.

"What do you want to be when you grow up?"

"A joyful, enlightened being, shining with the inner light of a million stars."

"Go to your room."

How does it happen? How do you end up thinking you can and should know all about yourself and your future? The answer is found within that question about what you want to be. I know my parents would have reacted differently depending on whether I said "I want to be a prima ballerina" or "a math teacher" or "a bus driver" or whatever else. For you, your caregivers' responses taught you a lot about who you were supposed to become, and even who you were supposed to be then, as a kid. Your parents' reactions to what you *loved* gave you a context for what is appropriate or inappropriate for you to *be* and what is the right thing for you to want to do.

So you might have grown up feeling like you always needed to know (or should know) who you wanted to be. You didn't! You might even have believed that you should always be sure about who you are now. No need! It's ironic that a lot of us never have an *actual* answer to the "When you grow up" question, and I, for one, have not even grown up yet! But that's a different story. You don't need to decide what you're going to be. You don't need to decide what you are. You don't need to know the future. You don't need to know the present. You don't need to explain or excuse yourself for loving what you love.

There is the idea that you *can* know the future. And then there is the idea that you *should*. Let's forget both of those.

Many of us were trained to need a good excuse for everything. Having an excuse is like knowing the future. If you aren't careful, you can live under a constant pressure that what you're doing needs to make sense somehow, or be leading to a "better" or "right" life. The truth is, none of us knows what we're doing! We rarely have good excuses! (And many of us, you included, don't know what the heck a good excuse even looks like!) You have some ideas about how to live that you've picked up along the way, for sure, but that is a far cry from being able to predict the future and live your life in a *right, perfect* way. Yes, you have loves and hobbies and impressions and clues about who you are, but that isn't the same as knowing. Sometimes we think we know what we're doing, but it's just an illusion. And that's good news! No one yet has been able to wave a wand and see into the future. And I, for one, wouldn't want that power. I find it exciting that we don't know what will happen. And life gets a lot more fun when we stop trying to have the answers all the time. I certainly have more fun when I stop trying to have an always ready perfect excuse for my own existence. You can start really enjoying life when you stop trying to know what to do and whom to be all the time.

Being yourself is not about having a good excuse for being alive. It's not about getting things right, or feeling like you are the right kind of person. The process of discovery called being you is about something else altogether. Being you might be messy, and it usually brings up a lot more questions than it answers. Being you will sometimes complicate things. And I'm glad it will! Because, just like when you come to terms with not knowing the future, when you have a lot of questions and uncertainty while being yourself, you can have fun. You can enjoy this exciting trip called life. You are a wild, weird, fascinating human who is also, at your core, unpredictable. So it would make sense that you *don't* always make sense. K?

Draw a picture of what you really wanted to be when you grew up. Don't draw the right answer you were supposed to tell everybody, but what you truly wished for as a kid.

What's the difference between the person in the drawing and yourself today? If the person in the drawing could tell you something about who you are today or maybe give you advice, what would they say? Write their words below . . .

• • •

People don't ever wake up one day, having found themselves, and declare the quest over. This "finding" isn't a single event like finding a lost shoe. It is a becoming, an ongoing process of discovery. And that's okay. It's more than okay, actually, it's great. Believe it or not, you wouldn't want it to be too short or too easy. In a way, that would take the fun out of the discovery. How do we live? How do we love? How do we hate? What do we like? What do we dislike? The good news is that once you've found answers to those questions, you might discover that if you start at the beginning of the list of questions again, all of your answers will have changed! I guess what I'm trying to say is that you need not be surprised if "not knowing" is a lifelong process. What you're hoping for, what you're yearning for, is the questioning, not *to find the answers*. And to be frank, answers are boring. In fact, I very much hope you never find solid answers about your deepest truths. I hope you can discover more questions about yourself as you keep growing (or never grow up). Your life at fifteen, thirty-five, and eighty-five years old needs as much care and openness to discovery as your life at five years old.

I know you get the idea sometimes that you are supposed to be moving toward some solid state in life. Like you're moving toward the moment of your year or your lifetime when you have it all figured out. I have a very important question for you: Then what happens? So you've done it. Whatever it is, you've done it. You've done the thing or found out info about yourself that puts you in an "I have it all figured out" state of mind, and . . . then what happens to you? Do you die right there? Or perhaps you live happily ever after? Or . . . what? I have news for you. You can spend your life trying to reach that someday when you've got it all figured out, or you can start to enjoy this life you have right now with all the uncertainty and questioning. What are you supposed to do? How are you going to get there? What have you done recently to make all that happen? What do you want to be when you grow up? To all of which you can answer, "Oh, I dunno."

#DearJeffrey

Half the time I feel like a mess.
I don't know what I'm doing or what I'm
supposed to be like. Everybody else has it
all together. Why can't I be like that?

I'd like to share a secret confession that most people don't like to talk about. Before I get to that, I want everybody to know that this book is *for* everybody. It is for every kind of person, especially all ages of people. But because of what I'm trying to do here, I need to talk often about what it's like to be a kid. When we're kids we get fed this lie that adults know what they're doing—that adults do know the future. It sounds crazy! To keep us in line, or to keep us believing the status quo, or to keep us behaving, we're led to believe that older people know everything, or certainly more than we, the younger people, do. It's not necessarily the case. And that's the secret confession that a lot of adults don't like to tell kids. Adults have more *experience* than kids, yes. Maybe they've been living in the "real world" longer than teens have, for example. But that doesn't always mean they know best, and it doesn't always mean that adults shouldn't listen to the ideas and the wisdom of kids. I can remember being a kid and knowing that to be gender different, to be queer, was perfectly okay, while a lot of the adults around me "knew" I was flawed and damaged and needed fixing and changing. I can remember feeling invisible, feeling resentful, because I was never consulted about how I wanted to live my own life. The message I got was change and become "normal," or *else*.

To address your question specifically, we're all a mess. What makes us even more of a mess is that when it comes to relating to one another, adults sometimes spend too much time trying to hide the fact that they are a mess as well. To me, there's nothing wrong with being a mess, and if more older people were just willing to be open about how they don't actually know what the heck is "right" or best, I think we'd all get along better. Adults can't predict the future. Adults can't stop things from happening that hurt the people they love. Adults are just as out of control and just as much of a mess as anyone. So, in short, I want to encourage all of us to stay a big mess. And we need to be open about the messes we are. Please don't conform and try to get things right and "have it all figured out." First, that's impossible, and second, it's a total waste of time. As hard as you try to maintain an image of not being a big mess, you are always confronted with the reality that you are just a big mess anyway. And that's great news! Because being a mess doesn't have to mean what you think it means.

Everybody else doesn't "have it all together." Not by a long shot. We are all learning. We are all changing, sometimes in ways we like and sometimes in ways we don't like. The more I learn, the more I realize that there's a whole lot I don't know. And that's perfectly fine.

Related to knowing, you were also trained to try to find your "purpose in life." That seems to be a universally accepted quest, even a noble way to spend a life, *but nobody seems to know exactly what that means.* "Finding your purpose" can be confusing in the same way that "being yourself" is; the more you know, the worse off you are. I am all for everybody finding and then doing something that they love, but could it be possible, just possible, that, for all of us, our purpose in life is just to be fabulous and enjoy our time? Does that sound selfish or lazy? Maybe, but a lot of us seem to "know" (mistakenly) that our true purpose is something like pleasing other people or doing what makes our parents happy, or something along those lines. And even if you're past that, even if you see the futility of trying to live your life impressing or pleasing other people, you can still get caught in this incredible swirl of anxiety about not having yet found your mysterious purpose in life. The answer? Stop trying. Get used to not knowing.

That may sound easy for me to say. I'm making videos, I'm advocating for youth. *I already know my purpose!* But wait, don't be so sure . . . because I'm not. I love what I do. And some of it is wildly successful and some of it flops, and what keeps me going is not a surety that I have *found my purpose.* What keeps me going is that I love what I'm doing. And, by the way, to borrow another confusing phrase, have I "found myself"? Has doing any of this helped me find my true self? Heck no! What does that mean? In actuality, I'm the one who isn't sure about anything but is thoroughly enjoying trying all kinds of interesting stuff. That is so different from "having it all figured out" and "knowing who I am" and "having a purpose in life" and whatever other nonsense we can think of that suggests that this isn't one big, giant, creative, make-it-up-as-we-go-along mess. And, you get to enjoy that mess! Please enjoy not knowing. Please enjoy your unsettled, crazy, unconventional life. You get to experiment with what it means to find yourself and maybe even begin to lose yourself in the constant, wild, and constantly wild process of not knowing. You can stop the madness of needing to have an excuse or a good reason or a purpose *for being* and just enjoy your life.

In the long run, I think it is better for you not to be so sure about who you are. I do get asked *all the time,* "How are you so confident?" In this context, the answer is an ironic one: I have gotten more and more comfortable and confident because I know that I *do not know* who I am. I have gotten comfortable with the uncomfortable feeling of not knowing.

Hero/ine

Ruth Bader Ginsburg is the first Jewish woman justice on the Supreme Court. She has fought for the advancement of women's rights throughout her career. She has always experimented with how she "should" be and has brought her exploration to her interpretation of the law, allowing each case she has tried to stand on its own merits instead of assuming how the people involved should act based on other people's actions or opinions.

When Ruth went to Harvard Law School, she was one of nine women in a class of five hundred, and the dean of Harvard at the time asked her one day to explain to some of her classmates why she was occupying a place in class that he knew could be occupied by a man. Ruth has never said how she reacted in that moment, but we do know she didn't take what the dean "knew" at face value. Should a man be there in her place? She would find out. Ruth continued attending classes, and was eventually ranked first in her class at Harvard.

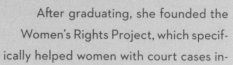

After graduating, she founded the Women's Rights Project, which specifically helped women with court cases involving discrimination. You could say that the Women's Rights Project helped to undermine what a lot of people thought they knew about how women should behave. Ruth said she founded the Project to "go after the stereotypes that were written into law." In one of the Women's Rights Project's first cases before the Supreme Court, *Frontiero v. Richardson* in 1973, Ruth herself said, "Sex [Gender], like race, has been made the basis for unjustified, or at least unproved, assumptions concerning an individual's potential to perform or to contribute to society. These distinctions have a common effect: They help keep woman in her place, a place inferior to that occupied by men in our society." What people knew about women was challenged.

Ruth kept exposing false beliefs throughout her career. In addition to her detractors, Ruth has many fans who appreciate her way of disputing long-held beliefs and assumptions. It was recently announced in a national poll by Public Policy Polling that Ruth ranked first for people choosing their favorite Supreme Court justice.

It's not only that knowing or thinking you know is dangerous. It's what you *do* with what you think you know that can cause a lot of suffering. When you know how you should be, you also tend to assume that how you are now is not the way you should be. In other words, if you're like most people, you have built a whole life on the belief that there is a right way you should be. And if it isn't obvious, that belief goes hand in hand with the thought that however you are right now isn't the right way you should be. If you didn't know there was a right way to be, you also wouldn't know that you aren't being that right way. The two thoughts work together. That whole way of framing your life is a trap. Both statements are linked and both statements are false.

As an example, let's come back to confidence. It seems overwhelmingly true, at least in my line of work, that people think confident is the right way to be and that if they are being shy it's the wrong way to be. People see me as confident and want to be like me because they think that's the right way to be. I sometimes answer their question "How can I be confident like you?" in the same way: try being confident if you want to, but have you also considered that shy is a great way to be too?

Earlier, we looked at a #DearJeffrey question about confidence. Maybe a lot of people message me with that question because they wish they could have the freedom that I seem to (and do!) have. I seem to know who I am and act with a surety and bravado because of it. Maybe people wish they could boldly and beautifully be themselves, like they assume I'm being. Well, here's my take on the whole thing. Don't assume you know that how you are is wrong. Don't stop being shy if you're naturally shy. Don't stop being a diva if you're naturally a diva. Also practice this: don't assume that how you are is not something natural and healthy for you. You could be a genuinely thoughtful, introspective shy person. (I'm not like that, but *you* could be!) And, guess what? The world needs that from you. Make a point to offer to the world what you are. This is where getting comfortable with the unknown comes in. Saying "I don't know" gives you a split second—a tiny bit of time—to just be however you are. Stop trying to be the way you "know" you should be. If you take one thing from this book, please let it be this: *I am not encouraging anyone to become more like me. I am encouraging everyone to become more like themselves.*

If you are shy, love your shyness. If you are bold, love your boldness. If you suspect your shyness or boldness actually comes from a fearful hiding of who you are, then find safe ways to experiment with being another way. Stop knowing and start experimenting! Find out for yourself. Don't trust what you were taught or what you think you know. I am never going to talk about a certain single quality that is better than another quality. I will always talk about the process of finding a way for you to safely and kindly be whatever it is you are naturally. And perhaps (I'll say it again here) if you are unsure about who you are naturally, that's wonderful! You have a wide-open space in which to explore.

It takes some guts to give up on the things you know about how you are supposed to be, but, speaking as a person who has taken that plunge, who has gone ahead and opened up the gift that is experimenting with who I am, I can say it's totally worth it. In fact, I couldn't imagine another way to be free, if freedom is something you're after. You can be your shy or not shy self, or you can be some natural way in between shy and not. You can be confident on Tuesday, and not on Wednesday through Friday. You can experiment with not knowing. And by the way, the negative consequences that you might fear of an experiment like this are minuscule. You can experiment in a way that feels kind and safe for you, and you'll likely discover that the rewards are frequent and delightful. One of my favorite experiments is to wear something "I would never" wear. If you loosen up, you get to play and have a bit of fun with your life. And besides, it is a bit dull to remain a carbon copy, always "right" person. The time has come to step out of that old story of you and into a new role. Stop knowing. The time has come for you to belong. Maybe not all at once, maybe more bit by bit, but you deserve to be yourself, whatever the heck that means!

Remember, the more you think you know about who you are supposed to be, the more you will find out how wrong you are about yourself. It's natural. When you are sure of your identity, you're sometimes actually sure of other people's negative opinions of how inadequate you are or how you always "mess things up." So question what you know. Question authority.

Not knowing means different things to different folks. I hope you mostly take that phrase and this chapter as an invitation. It can be a big exploration. Hopefully it will open up a chance for you to feel included, to feel a bit more human. Instead of clinging to a notion of yourself from the long past (some way you know is the right way for you to be), you can get more and more current. You can try to see the fragility of the things that were taught to you. And you can even start to make changes to how you see yourself, not because you judge yourself but because you simply want to make changes. You will see the truth that you can handle whatever life brings you. Not knowing is okay, despite what adults taught you growing up. And you deserve to blossom in your life, instead of just trying to know everything.

8

...

FEEL GOOD

Feeling bad doesn't get you anywhere. A popular theory goes that if you do something "wrong," you will feel bad about it, and you are then persuaded not to do that wrong thing again. That's actually a crazy theory. Why in the world do you need the middle step of feeling bad? Can't you just live your life and see when something doesn't work, then do your best not to do that thing again? So you say something unkind because you're in a bad mood, or you forget totally about doing your homework, or you really don't want to do any homework ever again for the rest of your life. Those are all normal things that humans do and feel from time to time. Is it really necessary for you to feel bad in order to change these behaviors? Can't you just notice that when you said the unkind thing, you hurt somebody else and you don't want to do that anymore? Done. Easy. Clean. You have been too convinced in too many situations to feel bad. Now it's time to feel good.

But instead of walking around feeling good, you are supposed to go into a shame spiral of "Why am I this way?" "If I keep insulting people I won't have any friends left!" "Why was I so stupid?" "If I don't do my homework I'll never graduate!" "What is wrong with me?" And on and on, all *supposedly* so that you can learn to never do whatever you did again.

But here's something I want you to consider:

You never *will* do that thing again. As far as I can tell, people never ever repeat the exact same conversations or situations in their lives. So feeling bad about yesterday's mistake isn't all that helpful because the exact situation will never happen the exact same way again. That is not to say that you won't find yourself in similar situations, and that you shouldn't learn or adjust or change. Of course you change and grow, whether you want to or not. That's what we constantly do. It would be silly to spend your life trying not to learn. But you don't need to feel bad in order to learn.

It is utter sadness if you were taught and brought up in a way that ties feeling bad to learning. You started out curious and bright and you asked a lot of questions. Then maybe someone in authority said something like, "Stop asking so many annoying questions." Or perhaps after you'd done something that wasn't very skillful, they laid on you the craziest, most upsetting time-machine-assuming confusing phrase on planet earth: "You should have known better." You learned to stop asking questions. Somewhere, whether from a teacher or parent or whoever, you got the idea that the way you are supposed to learn is by yourself and by feeling guilty when you've done a wrong thing. So . . . uh . . . this helps you learn and prevents you from doing the wrong thing again, right?

Couldn't you maybe find another way to learn that works just as well and doesn't require the guilt of feeling like you're a bad person because you screwed up again? Is life here to punish you into learning how to act in a way that you should? Is the whole point of life feeling bad so that you learn? Should you feel bad until you learn how you're supposed to act? This is a very little kid's way of looking at the world. And just so we're clear, eventually you can choose to grow up and *not feel bad about things.* This chapter will tell you how.

I know at first it might sound crazy—a little radical. How else are you going to learn if you don't feel bad? Well, how about this? I bet you could try just observing and trusting your own instincts and being kind to yourself when you do something you wish you hadn't. It's worth a shot at least!

#DearJeffrey

I feel like the only way I can learn is from my mistakes. And when I make mistakes, I feel bad. I mean, I don't like it, but sometimes I feel too stupid to learn just by looking around. And you say I shouldn't feel bad because there are no mistakes? How can I learn anything, then, if I don't acknowledge the mistakes I've made?

Before we get to the real answer, here's a related little treatise on the word *stupid:* it's stupid. People learn at a really early age to call things they don't like or don't understand stupid. And if someone calls you stupid, you need to challenge their assessment. If you call yourself stupid, you *really* need to challenge that assessment because *stupid* is a relative term that most people use as a stand-in word for what . . .

unacceptable? Wrong? You are certainly not those things. I'm going to reword the question slightly and think of it like this: "I don't know if I'm wise enough to learn unless it's by making a bunch of mistakes and then feeling bad about them." Fair enough.

When something bad happens because of something you've done, if you think of that as a mistake, you are buying into this weird, impossible notion I mentioned earlier that you *should have known better*. You can't know better, because if you had, you would have done better in the first place (or shall we say you would have done something differently?). There are no time machines. You're not psychic. No one can know better *before* something happens.

The idea that you need to feel like something is your fault (like you did something wrong) in order to learn is another issue and it is so incredibly horrible. If you were taught that lie, you deserve a Medal of Awesomeness, because to live with that belief is difficult indeed. To keep going in a world where the outcomes of the brand-new situations and things you do are an ultimate sign of your worth as a person is really an unfortunate life on a torture farm. You live under so much weight every day when you think you need to know better and control the outcomes of things you can't control in order to prove your worth. So in order to cut off feeling bad before it starts, you'll need to give up on the idea that it's possible to know better *before a decision is made.* When you notice that you've made an unfortunate choice or decision, ask yourself, "Didn't I make the best choice I could with the information I had at the time?"

You'll make unfortunate choices. Yes. Things will go in ways that you wish they hadn't sometimes. Yes. There is no magic formula (and no chapter in this book!) that offers you the ability not to make some choices you'll wish you hadn't made in your life. It happens to everyone. It's not possible to avoid it. What I'm talking about is how to treat yourself when those things do occur. Is it useful or helpful to feel bad because of the supposed mistakes you've made? No.

This idea of giving up feeling bad is exciting because what will you focus on instead of feeling bad? What will become the focus of your life if you someday just stop spending so much time thinking about avoiding making mistakes? What will you think about instead? What will you do with all your time? Will you fly to the moon or start a political movement? Become a doctor? Clean your house? The possibilities are endless. And the open-mindedness is endless. And you know what? When your mind is way open like that, when you don't have to worry about whether you've done it all wrong and whether you have made a mistake, you are in the perfect place to actually learn. You are in the perfect spot to really see what you need to see and do what you need to do. You can take whatever action there is to take without fear and without the idea of "mistakes" hanging over you. You can be really free. Sounds amazing, right?

Most people are so invested in the idea that feeling bad works that they haven't stopped to notice that it really actually *doesn't* work. I post positive things on the Internet. "There is nothing wrong with you. There is no reason to feel bad about who you are." On said Internet, because of Godwin's law, I get asked a million times a day, "What about Hitler? Won't we all turn into Hitler if we don't feel bad for our mistakes?" Why is the Internet so obsessed with Hitler? I think what's really behind the Hitler question is, if I don't feel bad about making a mistake, won't that lead to me making even bigger mistakes? If people are totally free to act *however*, won't they act in horrible ways? Some will and some won't. In this book we're focused on you. If you prove to yourself that there's no such thing as a mistake in this way, that you don't need to feel bad in order to learn from your experiences, I think you'll be happy, not genocidal! You simply can recognize that there are valuable lessons to be gleaned from your actions and the results. A better question to ask is, why in the world do people punish themselves internally as if they *were* Hitler? Why are we so severe with ourselves? Why do we punish ourselves at all? Why do we walk around thinking we deserve to feel bad?

Our main question here is, is there an alternative to feeling bad that works? And the answer is yes. There are a million possibilities of how we can learn without shame and guilt. And there are a million ways to just feel good. We are not only giving up on feeling bad; we are going all the way over into feeling good. If you are refusing to feel bad, you will have time and energy to do things that make you feel good. As a matter of fact, it might be helpful for you to sit down and list all the things you love to do—things that support you to feel good. Here are a few of my favorites to get your list started.

Ways to Feel Good

 Move Around

This one is essential. You have to free up the energy in your body. Every morning I start with a four-mile brisk walk. I do at least that much every day because when I don't I feel the difference, I start to feel bad. I start to feel like something's stuck, and moving around really frees things up. You should do whatever physical activity you enjoy as often as you need to feel good.

Hero/ine

Dr. Brené Brown has studied feeling bad and its effect on people's lives. She is one of the most respected researchers on the outcomes of feeling shame, and she is now a research professor at the University of Houston Graduate College of Social Work. In her very popular TED talk from 2010 called "The Power of Vulnerability" she discusses how a willingness to be vulnerable gives you a chance to transcend shame and leave behind feeling bad about yourself.

She has written many books on vulnerability, worthiness, courage, and shame, including a book called *Rising Strong*. In it she says: "If we are brave enough, often enough, we will fall. This is a book about what it takes to get back up."

She is the founder of an organization called The Daring Way, which helps bring all she's learned in her research about how to avoid shame and feel good to churches, schools, and families.

Do Something Creative

Art project!! What's your hobby? What do you collect or make that helps you to feel really proud? What you're going for here is a sense of accomplishment. Pick some small project or projects that you can enjoy doing, but that you can also be proud of afterward (anything from stamp collecting or building model trains to painting your bedroom a new color or organizing your sock drawer). Whether you're learning as you go or you're already excellent at your project, remember to celebrate your work after you're done.

 Volunteer

Be around like-minded people. You could always help humans or animals that need you. I often feel a sense of belonging and community when I'm with people who care about the same things I do. Volunteering makes me feel valued and like I'm making a difference. Go lick some envelopes.

Meditate

As we've talked about a few times in this book, an excellent way to feel good is to (re)connect with yourself. Meditation or a similar practice helps you be still enough to remember what's most important, even if it's just for a short time each day. It helps you to feel good. You can find instructions online, in many great books, or even at a community center near where you live.

 Eat Good Food

It can feel good to eat your favorite thing. If that fave thing isn't exactly healthy, it's okay to have it every once in a while. But for feeling good more often, you want to consciously pick foods that are good for your body. Get your veggies going. What you put on your plate is not just nourishment; it's a signal to you and your body of how much you care. Eat and feel good.

Listen to Your Favorite Music

You love Broadway soundtracks for a reason! Why not spend more time listening to them? This goes for reading your favorite books and watching movies that you really like. It's nice to take some time and enjoy something that speaks to you.

Clean Your Room

For my teen readers, this is a real suggestion. I swear your parents didn't pay me to say this! A clean space can feel like a cared-for space, and when you care for your apartment or house or wherever you are, it's almost like the space itself feels good. And who doesn't like that?

Talk to People Who Love You

Call somebody, would you? Now, I get it, your relationship with your family can be complicated, so maybe you pick a different friend you'll call or see each week "just 'cause." Connecting this way helps you see yourself through their eyes and immerse yourself in the familiarity of your connection. Losing touch with friends can make you feel lousy and like you've made some kind of mistake, so stay in communication. Enjoy your time together.

GOOD ENOUGH

Create a Good Enough to Feel Good list
all about you.

Write on it all the ways you can think of that
you are good.

What are your best qualities?

TO FEEL GOOD

How are you helpful and kind?

List your talents and strengths.

What do you offer the world?

Hang your list somewhere where you can add to it every day.

I suspect we keep feeling bad even when it doesn't work for a couple of reasons: (1) we keep thinking it will get us somewhere and, worst of all, (2) it's simply familiar. Feeling bad is how we've always done it. But can't you see? You don't learn (or at least learn well) that way. It's actually really hard to change something just because you feel bad and know you "should" change. Most of us actually don't change if this is the method we're using. So I want to share the way out of feeling bad, or at least what worked for me and what I hope will have some relevance for you as you experiment with this whole thing for yourself. Drumroll . . .

Just. Don't. Do. It.

Surprise! It's totally that simple. One day I just gave it a try. Refused to go there. No magic, no method really. I just thought, *I'm going to stop feeling bad*, and I went for it. I looked for times and places where I would normally feel bad about something I had done, and I tried not feeling bad. Now, reducing the whole process down to a couple of sentences makes it seem easy, or like it should be easy. It wasn't. It was quite hard actually. It took focus and dedication and a whole lot of reminding and forgetting and recommitting. It was a big deal and it took a long time. But, as you might be suspecting at this point, it really paid off. Not feeling guilt or shame can be a struggle from time to time still, but being on the other side of the experience, I can absolutely say that it is worth any amount of effort imaginable to kick the habit. You can get a coach, or check in with someone you love (tell them to help you with not feeling bad anymore), and find support in any way you need to. You're not alone and this is absolutely something you can do. It won't happen in a snap, but it sure seems like something you can at least try (if not get really good at) doing.

Nobody needs to accept what I say at face value, by the way. I really didn't write this book so that you would automatically listen to me. Find out for yourself. Try feeling bad for a week and then try not feeling bad. What's the difference? Which one do you like better? I'm not joking! Maybe I missed something. Does feeling bad have some great benefit I'm not aware of? You try it. And while you're trying it, give yourself time and a little space.

ON-CAMERA QUESTIONING

As I blossomed into a self-accepting adult, I never forgot how I felt on the playground. . . . I never forgot, even while I was at work being famous, what it's like to live a life of feeling bad for who you are and what you've done.

And yet I did need to act fearlessly. Shoving a mic in a stranger's face takes more than a little gumption. When I filmed my first candid interviews for TV, I didn't realize that being asked to step up and interact in that way would be a sticky, emotional, fearful place for me. I was afraid of making a mistake and I had no idea how un-confident I would feel. Cameras were there, I was all dressed up cute, and my stomach was churning, my chest was fluttering. I was a mess! At the time, I thought maybe forcing people to talk would make them feel bad. Then I would feel bad for making them feel bad! I knew that not everyone loves to be a star like I do, not everyone wants to be spotlighted.

Of course, the crew *asks* people if they want to be interviewed, and people are told what to expect. But I still had my doubts as the segment producer and camera crew and I wandered the streets of sunny Santa Monica, California, looking for interviewees. I was super unsure inside, ready to feel bad at a moment's notice. Would people be too nervous to talk? Would they be turned off by my look, overcome with jealousy over my gorgeous long legs in my short shorts and Manolo pumps? Would they bristle at the questions we'd prepared? And worst of all, would I say the wrong thing? Would I offend someone? I had been taught to take things personally, to feel bad just for existing sometimes, and this was a doozy of a chance to practice not feeling bad. I was more than a little nervous, not sure what would come next, believing that, just like I felt earlier in life, I was gonna blow it. I was going to make a big mistake.

I really recommend you become a TV star. The thing about being a sparkling, have-it-all-together TV personality is this: it really requires you to make the transition from worshipping heroes to becoming one. TV requires you to go from obsessing over what other people think and whether you'll make a mistake to valuing your inner shine. When I got in front of the camera, there was a job to do, and whatever drama was going on for me internally needed to be paused for a moment. Don't get me wrong! This, especially this, is a job I love, and the freedom of being myself on camera is like no other. But being on camera is also a great responsibility. It sure isn't a place to allow self-doubts and judgments and fears to creep in. I used to think that heroes were people who didn't have self-judgment and doubt. I steadily learned that heroes might have all the doubt in the world, they just *set it aside and act anyway.* And refusing to feel bad no matter what happens sure comes in handy.

I was glad to have my fears and doubts proven useless that day. Most people we asked went beyond just being willing to be interviewed. They were open. They were honest. I didn't expect it, but interviewing strangers on the street was a breeze. Nothing to fear! Nothing to feel bad about. People seemed eager to be heard and appreciated, and they also seemed eager to share the wisdom they'd collected. Everybody wants to talk about their hard-learned lessons and their joyful truths, their struggles when they might have felt bad, and their paths to growth. Few of us are full-fledged champions or heroes in our lives until we've learned some hard lessons. And few of us are true heroes in the world until we work to undo the guilt and shame in ourselves and others.

One more tiny warning: you might find (as often happens when you start to change things in your life) that the people you hang around with would prefer you not change. It seems strange, but the people around you might prefer it if you kept feeling bad. I wanted to provide this little warning. When I started not feeling bad, people who were really invested in feeling bad themselves (the people who think it really works) got super mad at me and tried everything they could think of to get me to feel bad again. Good thing I wasn't having that!

So fair warning, this isn't just a personal thing you're doing; it will affect others, but probably it will affect the people you know in a positive way the most. I will say that the majority of the time, when I decided not to feel bad, people took that as an escape hatch for themselves. They seemed grateful. I don't think any of us could have articulated it, but I suspect that when I was free of that "feel bad to become a better person" garbage, it gave other people a little glimmer of light, of hope, that it's possible for them to stop feeling bad too.

When *you* do it, that's when you'll become a walking, breathing example of not feeling bad for other people. I've done it and I can report that the decisions I make and the relationships I have and the things I learn are so much nicer, so much richer, so much better, than anything I "learned" because I felt guilty or bad about something. This is a radical idea. This will be a lifetime of finding out and trying and growing away from the punishing, useless internal hate of feeling bad, but, as I said before, you're totally worth the effort.

What's one issue in your life that makes you feel bad? Consider how your life would be if you didn't feel this way anymore. What would change? Use this space to draw a picture or write a paragraph about your life minus the need to feel bad about this issue.

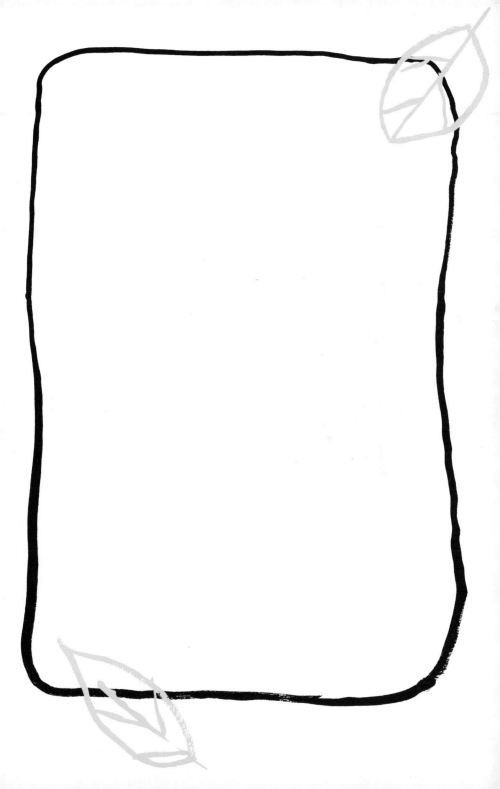

9
. . .
STAY CONNECTED TO YOU

While living in Philadelphia, I would visit a local spiritual bookstore from time to time. I found the smell of incense and the prismatic shine from the hanging crystals intoxicating. And they had a wall with what seemed like a million dream catchers! I didn't know why I liked that place so much, it just kinda felt like somewhere I belonged somehow. As a poor farm kid in the Big City, I found the whole store exciting and exotic. One day, from across the room, a book title jumped out at me, *There Is Nothing Wrong with You* by Cheri Huber. When I read the title I thought, *No. That can't be right.* But of course, deep down, I knew it was. I recognized the truth of it, even though I couldn't say so. Reading that book was the first step on a path of lifelong spiritual seeking that would lead me to study Zen at a monastery in California. Over the years, that book and the teachings from which it sprang have helped me to be here, now.

Ultimately, it is your *job* to stay connected to yourself. Your job is to stay connected to the truth we've been talking about in this book. Unlike the usual "day job," this one can be a joyous experience, and, in fact, that's part of how it works: You learn to take care of yourself and you learn to enjoy life by doing so. You might have questions. You might have doubts. You might think it's impossible or that you aren't up to the task, but it isn't and you are. And again, you can enjoy it.

A popular roadblock here is thinking that it's someone else's responsibility. It's popular to think that your job is to really stay connected to someone else—to stay connected to what the kids at school or your friends at work think of you. I want to ask you to stay connected to *your* truth, to your heart. You might at some point think it is up to an author or guru or pastor to make you happy—to get you out of the terrible loops we all sometimes find ourselves in, but it's not. It is up to you. The good news is it's always been up to you. And I want to tell you how to get started with that. But let's be clear about one more thing first: you might at some point think the job of taking care of your emotional needs is totally up to your parents, that they should have taught you differently or even that they should offer you (right now, as a teen or adult) what you need to be happy. You might think that's *their job*. It's not their job. Even the best parent has times when they can't take care of our needs, and parents are people too—sometimes they are having trouble finding happiness for themselves as well. And that's okay. This isn't an indictment of parents because this isn't a problem. This is simply how it seems to work. The only person who can take lasting, loving lifelong care of you is you. The only reason I bring it up here, toward the end of our time together, is that it would be a shame for you to wait. Don't wait on your parents or your friends. Don't wait to strengthen and practice that connection with yourself. Don't wait for that guru. Don't wait for an outside hero. You can't wait. You can't afford to wait. The time is now to get connected, and stay connected, to you.

To sit this one out, to take a passive attitude toward your own happiness, is not just a waste of time, it's deadly. Don't waste your whole life waiting for your life to begin! And all this time you're spending expecting other people to do this growing, this opening, this learning, *for you*, you are suffering. You might even get bitter. You might get sad. You might think that because Mom or your pastor can't offer the acceptance you need, you truly are unacceptable. You might start to think that there is no hope for you. But, of course, there is hope for you. There is hope for everyone. And the hope is found in learning what helps you feel supported and safe and giving that to yourself. The hope is in learning how to connect and reconnect and reconnect again to your own inner wisdom. I've given you some tools, but now it's up to you to use them and find new tools and take it all to heart. This isn't magic. And happiness and fulfillment aren't going to come from some outside savior. They are your responsibility and the answers lie within you.

#DearJeffrey

Sometimes I feel really down and discouraged, like the world has really gotten to me. I hate that feeling. What can I do to stop feeling that way?

It seems crazy but the best way to stop feeling that way is to really *let* yourself feel that way. The only way out is through. So much of this book and so much of "how to be you" lies in giving yourself permission to be however you are. We are sentient beings and that's what we do: we feel. Like we talked about in our chapter on emotions, people often assume that certain kinds of feelings are bad, or that they've done something wrong if they feel sad or down. That's far from true. Really. Everybody seems to get down sometimes. Everybody seems to get happy sometimes. As far as I can tell, it's all part of being a human. So why in the world would you assume that you shouldn't feel any way you feel? Why are you avoiding something that's perfectly natural?

A few times I've outlined a pretty common pattern: you are some natural way and, with time and social pressure, you start to think that your natural way is bad or wrong. And the whole point of this book is that *people* aren't wrong. *Feelings* aren't wrong. Life isn't out to get you. *You are not wrong.* So many of your ideas about who you are come at first from outside you, but then from inside your head. So much suffering happens because of the way you learned to think—the thoughts in your brain. I would say that you get down only because of the conversation in your head. You get down because, by and large, there is a long, terrible, argumentative stream of thoughts in your head that (as crazy as it sounds) is telling you who you are and how you should be. This inner conversation is interpreting the world around you pretty much every waking moment.

The great thing is that if you can learn to quiet the voice in your head, if you can learn to pay attention to something else, you might start to hear . . . life. You might connect to yourself in a way you never have. This crazy inner arguing and nasty, unfriendly voice in your head saying, "Well, that was stupid," could be replaced with the sounds of the street as you walk or your favorite music. Some folks I know have actually been really successful at using loving recordings of their own voice to replace the hateful messages in their heads. (Read about their work, called *Recording and Listening*, at recordingandlistening.org.) It's not easy to do, but it's possible. Staying connected to yourself and your heart is a big part of this process. In order to be happy, you must learn to rely less on that conversation in your mind and put your attention on the present— on your heart— on the world around you. You must start to listen to life and not listen to the judgments and self-hate in your head. What can you do to be present to what's happening right now? How do you tell the difference between hateful programming you got as a kid and the wisdom from your heart? I'll tell you.

When someone says, "Listen to your heart," you might have several reactions:

What does that mean?

That sounds stupid.

That is so hokey, it's almost meaningless.

I've been waiting for this. That's what I always wanted to hear.

These are some ways to recognize messages from your heart. Your heart is never judgmental. To me, the heart doesn't even speak in words, it's almost like it speaks in impulses and senses. You will certainly get some profound truths and deep insights when you listen to your heart, but it probably won't happen in complete, definitive statements. That other, mental conversation, the self-hating one that you were taught as a kid to take from the outside to the inside, is full of clear, definitive statements: You shouldn't have done that. You're too fat. You ruined that friendship.

The heart, on the other hand, is poetic and kind. The heart is warm. It's a feeling of being okay. It's a realization that you belong. The heart automatically sees the best in you. The heart acknowledges how far you've come and how far you want to go. Listening to the heart is a process of feeling understood, of finally connecting to the love you always wanted. You are not the sum of what happened to you in the past. Your present is not a cumulative, inevitable outcome of your past. You have choices about how you live right now, and you have choices about how you encounter yourself.

Here Are My Big Ideas About How to Keep Exploring

Learn to spend quality time alone.

This one is so important that I'm repeating it here. So much torture, so much worry, is brought into our lives by our inability to just sit still by ourselves. You can start slow. It can be anything, but you must find ways to be in silence and solitude. You can find time to get to know yourself that way. You can find time for you to be just you. *I'm talking about kind, open time.* Time spent worrying about what other people think of you and hating your "mistakes" isn't helpful and it's time you can never get back. Worry and hate are habits, and so are love and forgiveness. No matter how long it takes you, it is worth the effort to learn new habits, to teach yourself to love—to teach yourself to connect to you. Hopefully some of the exercises in this book have helped you practice these new habits. Now take them and run with them. Create your own exercises—your own lists of joy, your own dreams for yourself, your own interpretations of yourself and the world. The best advice I can give now is stick with it. Stay connected to you.

You shouldn't spend all of your time alone, of course. It is lovely to have friends! It is great to have a partner whom you love very much. Just know that neither of those things are the real deep-down thing you're looking for. Don't get me wrong! They are great, but they are a complement to (not a replacement for) your relationship with yourself.

It's likely that when you start to practice being alone and being okay with being alone, a lot will happen. You might feel intense things. You might have intense experiences. Or you might get bored. You might have boring experiences. Who knows what will be waiting for you! That's why it's perfectly okay to take it slow; why not start ultrasmall? Five minutes here, a little walk there. It's up to you what you do in your time with yourself. You can get used to this alone time and you can ramp things up as you find more ways and more times to enjoy yourself in solitude.

Forgive other people and yourself as best as you can.

Here is a tough one. Maybe this is the toughest. To me, there is nothing more important in forgiveness than an admission that everyone is doing their best. Letting go of the sins of others and your sins is a major step toward being free. You can't carry around the hurt and the exclusion and the anger and the sadness for the rest of your life. You mustn't. So how do you do it? How do you let go? You talk about things with someone you trust. You go to therapy. You live at a monastery if you think it will help. But all those things will hopefully bring you closer to self-acceptance. Just like anything else we've talked about in this book, the best method is to try things out and find out for yourself what works. And, of course, finding out is your responsibility. Friends and a therapist can help you, sure, but if you are unwilling to do the letting go for yourself, they can't help very much. This is not to blame anyone, it's just an observation: it will take work and it's worth it and you can surely do it.

What do you get when you let go and forgive others? You automatically let go and forgive what you have done. You are no longer a broken sinner and poorly equipped victim. You are powerful. You are the one in the best position to change your life. And when you do, you get freedom. You get to feel lighter, you get to walk with lightness and go places you never thought you deserved to go and talk to people you never dreamed you would. In the realization that the people from your past are okay, you see that you are okay, and you see that everyone is okay. And wouldn't you rather walk around with that on your mind than thinking about what everyone has done wrong? It's possible to retrain yourself to connect with your heart and not those internal judgments. And it is possible to install a new default of kindness and forgiveness and to live in a world of freedom.

Whatever your imagined crimes were in the past, they are not worth ruining your today for. You deserve to feel free. You deserve to be let off the hook. And as hard as it seems, you can let the people who taught you there is something wrong with you off the hook too. That may take a long time too—you may need to go to therapy or move to a monastery—but sooner or later you can make peace with the fact that everyone is doing their best. You can grow a little. Sometimes you work to forgive your neighbor or the friend who hurt you. And sometimes you are just growing up coming to see your parents as humans like you.

Do not give up.

It can be easy to get discouraged. It can be easy to feel like all this work isn't worth it. It can be hard to stick with unlearning what you have been taught about yourself and relearning the truth of who you are. I understand that. But this process of self-discovery can also be fun. The more you do it, the more fun it can be. If you feel like you don't want this book to end, start over and reread it. This process does get better. It does get easier. And although that might be little consolation right now, it is still true. We are in this together. There are people like you out there. And we are waiting for you. Your heart is waiting for you. You can go to jeffreymarsh.com and join our conversation. You can come out right now and join the fun.

This is what makes a good hero or heroine. It's not strength so much as it is willingness. It's not courageousness exactly; it's accepting *whatever* is going on. To me, that's a real hero. Nobody needs to have superstrength or save the planet from a million evil-doers. You just need to learn to be okay with yourself. There is magic in learning to be okay with yourself. And it might be the hardest thing a person can do! We are so trained, we think we see so much "evidence" about how awful we are. But we're not. You're not. And can you admit that to yourself? Are you willing to train yourself to see your own goodness, your innocence? Can you practice noticing your willing, creative moments? Can you get on board with a kind life, where you treat yourself as you would treat someone you love? Gosh, I hope so. And I hope that you can help anybody else who wants to do the same.

Imagine the Valentine you always wanted to receive. Draw that Valentine here. Use as much ribbon and glitter as you'd like. Get creative. List your best qualities. Tell yourself why you're so lovable. No one's watching. Don't hold back.

This book is not just for you. They don't know it yet, but this book is also for everyone you run into, everyone you know. When you start to find the willingness to let go of your past, when you start to accept and embrace and even love the person you are now, things change. When you find being loving to yourself and staying connected to yourself more important than being perfect or getting it right or having a ton of friends or being "successful," you are free. You don't just enjoy your own freedom, you are in a position to pass it on. If you get tired, if you get scared, maybe it will be helpful to remember that other people, whether they know it or not, are counting on you. They will benefit from the changes you make because they will (most of the time) recognize in you the changes *they can make* in themselves. Isn't that cool? So you grow for you. You grow for the team. You grow for everyone.

Hero/ine

You

The hero/ine is you.

You have been trying hard and doing your best to be a good person for a long while now. The time has come to acknowledge your own hard work. Maybe it's time to make a list of all the sacrifices, the pain, the money spent, and the hours given in the process of becoming the best you possible. Don't skip out on acknowledging your accomplishments! This is essential.

I didn't want to reveal this until the end of the book, but I *know* you're good. Only a truly good person would pick up a book like this and certainly only a really good person would read it all the way to the end. The reason I'm saying this is because you matter. We all matter. It might sound weird, but I want you to take a moment and let it sink in: you are a good person. Take some breaths. You are a good person. Relax your shoulders. You are a good person. Let go. You are a hero. You are capable of living a heroic life. You *are* living a heroic life.

APPENDIX

Ten Top Tips for Teachers
(and Anyone Who Works with Young People)

I work with young people. They write to me all the time. They message me about their experiences. They communicate. They respect me. And there are a few magical things I've learned about how to treat them. If you really want to reach young people, if you want to know what helps them feel safe and cared for and ready to learn from you as an educator or school administrator or camp counselor, read on.

1. Really Listen

Seems obvious, right? This is first because it is the most important. So many ills can be alleviated with concentrated respectful listening. You know deep down that you want to feel accepted and cared for and you want to feel like your opinions and experiences matter. The same is true for any student or young person you work with. Don't dismiss. Don't conflate. Don't belittle and don't rush any young person you're talking to. Take the care you would give to a close friend and give that to a student. Sit for a while. Pause before you respond. Really pay attention. Don't cut them off. *Listen*. Also, don't get all high and mighty. Assuming what someone means without actually asking for clarification is a big fat CDE: communication dead end. If you want a student to open up, then you need to do the work of showing them that it's safe to do so. Along these lines, please ask follow-up questions. Don't try to lead the conversation, but lean into it: "What do you mean? Can you say more about that?" Asking shows you care—it shows you're listening.

2. Get to Know the Lingo

One of the best ways to show respect to someone from a different background or generation is to understand the terms they use— especially when it comes to how they define themselves. Some of my fans' Twitter bios read like this: "I'm an a-romantic pansexual trans-fem DMAB." I realized at a certain point that I needed a vocab lesson if I was going to be of any use at all! In my day (which wasn't all that long ago) we didn't use any of these terms. I needed to "meet them where they were" if I was going to connect with and help any young person. So I learned. I asked around. I found out what the terms were, what folks in school were using to define themselves and their experiences of the world. Knowing what the vocabulary was went a long way to helping me show that I meant business and was ready to accept and respect whoever I was talking to.

3. Lobby for Safe Spaces (or Create Them)

This one might sound overly political and that's good news because it is overly political! Sometimes a teacher needs to be the one to advocate for the use of school space for clubs and gatherings that the school deems controversial or unimportant. Whether it's an LGBT or religious or just a hobby club, young people need at least one safe space to make connections with peers and find out they are not alone or freakish or as weird as they may be thinking. A safe space of this kind has several hallmarks. It is clean and respectful. It is private. It is free from other activities and groups. It is free from haters and bullies, whether they are students or teachers who disagree with what the club is offering. If a school refuses to allow a safe space that you know your students need, look for ways to assist with the club outside your school.

4. Take a Forthright Unequivocal Stand Against Bullying

In big and small ways, in your private life and in your public persona as an educator, you must take an antibullying stance. If any student senses an attitude of "Boys will be boys" or "Kids need to toughen up" or "It's not that big of a deal," you've already lost them. If you aren't willing to take a strong no-tolerance policy against bullying in your own school or classroom, you will never reach your students effectively. I'd recommend zero tolerance. If you witness bullying or you find out it's going on, you must show all the kids involved that bullying behavior has real (negative) consequences. Many schools have a structure in place for this kind of disciplinary action and my advice is to use that structure without hesitation. If you want to reach young people, you must be willing to respect them by keeping them physically and psychologically safe while they learn. Work to make your school's anti-bullying policy comprehensive. An appropriate policy should cover gender, race, sexual orientation, gender identity, and all the reasons that kids are bullied.

5. Treat Young People Like People

It feels kinda weird that I need to write that in a book, but there you go. I sometimes enjoy working with young people because they haven't learned to fake "having it all together" like adults have. None of us has it all together, and of course young'uns are going through the same stuff we all go through. There is a real beauty to how a young person sees things. When you're young, some things in life are sooooo dramatic and important. These are things that an adult might dismiss or oppress. Don't dismiss the student if they can't dismiss their drama. Young folks wear their heart on their sleeve—a lot of them don't have the social skills yet to avoid doing so. And I love that. Know for the purposes of this list that it's okay to assume that although a student may be caught up in the drama of something, the core experience is pretty much the same as your core experience.

6. Get Help If You Need It

Don't believe the lie that you need to do it all yourself. Just like I would tell a fan, you are not alone. There are a ton of organizations (GLSEN, for example) that love to help make schools safe for everyone. So Google for help. Reach out. Don't get caught up in thinking that communicating with and helping students is all up to you.

7. Be Honest. Be Real.

Here is where things get tricky. You want to maintain your privacy. Yes. It's often inappropriate to be totally honest with your students. Yes. As you've navigated what it means to be a teacher, you probably noticed a certain teaching-style spectrum in you and your colleagues. Some teachers are cold, distant, and authoritarian. Some act young and are chummy with their students. You likely avoid both of these extremes. But where does that leave you? When I say be honest, I mostly mean it is okay to drop the "I'm always right" authority-figure persona you might be tempted to use. You still need to lead the ship (that's part of your job, after all). I just wanted to point out here that really effective leaders often say, "I don't know," and "What do you think?" Stop putting up a wall between you and your students and talk directly to them. When I was a kid, I could always tell when a teacher was faking knowing all the answers. And the beauty is that you don't need to fake it. It's okay to be human. It's okay to try and fail. That is real strength. That is leadership.

8. Honor Their Experience

Just because you're older and probably wiser doesn't mean you're right. I think what bristles most young people is the double standard about their experiences in our culture. We tend to talk down to kids—not intentionally, but just out of habit. If you disagree with a student, try interacting with them as you would with an adult. For whatever reason, many teachers just tend to assume that a student's views and experiences are a little less valid than an adult's. Why do we do this? It seems basically arbitrary in most respects. Sure, a young person is less likely to have the depth and breadth of experiences that an adult has had, but that may not always be true. And if it is true, does it automatically mean that their opinions and experiences are somehow less valuable? Well . . . no.

9. Take Care of Your Own Issues

I'm going to word it as kindly as possible: you ain't gonna get out of this without learning to love yourself. You've got to go to therapy, start meditating, take some of the advice in this very book, if you're going to be of any help to others. It's really hard to teach someone to swim if you've never been in the water. Young people are vulnerable. They need someone who's been there and who can therefore help point the way forward. You have got to do the work yourself, and it is not only appropriate, it is necessary, to take the time to do that. To continue our metaphor, don't spend so much time teaching kids to swim that you lose your own enjoyment for swimming. Don't spend so much time helping others to swim that you have no time to "continuing ed" your own swim through life. It can feel cathartic to project all your stuff onto someone else and then go about accepting and caring for *them*, but it will fall flat and it will burn you out if you don't care for you. Learn to care deeply for you, and when your own cup of care runs over, care for others.

10. Give Yourself Some Credit

If you've read the rest of this book, you might have seen this coming. I totally tricked you. Someone who would read an appendix with this title, someone who cared enough to find out how to be a better teacher, is a good person. Admit it. Stop reading. Take a breath and *take that in*. This is the same stuff I tell my fans and followers. If only for just a moment, don't judge your performance as a teacher; don't get down about how you're not doing this "right." See yourself from the outside. Take note of how hard you're trying. Notice how hard the profession of teaching can be. And notice how deeply impactful you are every day. We all remember the teacher who inspired us, who was nice to us when we needed it, or who we felt really got us. You're changing lives, and it's totally okay to acknowledge your good hard work enthusiastically and often.

ACKNOWLEDGMENTS

It is imperative to have perspective in a process like this, and I am lucky to have Rick Sorkin's superb guiding voice for this book and my life. As a business manager, Rick has been a calming, equalizing presence and I could not have written this book or been able to affect so many lives without his astute and vivid direction. And, lucky me, he is also an incredibly good person and friend. Where does the advice-giver go when they need advice? To an insightful and keen, kind and trustworthy adviser. Rick Sorkin really understands me. He really accepts and supports all of me. Without his fierce enthusiasm for who I am and what I do, my career (and this book) would never have happened.

Cheri Huber has created an accessible and delightful approach to Zen Buddhist practice. Much of the lessons of this book have grown out of studying with her and Ashwini Narayanan, a student of Cheri's. Their integrous, intelligent and sincerely virtuous approach has inspired me. To further explore Cheri and Ashwini's writings, see *There Is Nothing Wrong with You*, *When You're Falling, Dive*, *What Universe Are You Creating?*, and *I Don't Want To, I Don't Feel Like It*. I cannot thank them enough for introducing me to a practice that has taught me how to accept and love all of what I am.

ACKNOWLEDGMENTS

As I mentioned in this book, they and their compatriots have created an excellent and effective practice called Recording and Listening. I love this idea and I do it every day. From recordingandlistening.org: "Spiritual practices have hundreds of recommendations for how we can train and practice paying attention. The practice of Recording and Listening is the one we recommend as the most powerful and transformative way of directly accessing the wisdom, love, and compassion that is our authentic nature. It is the most effective way we've found to learn to direct the attention." I couldn't agree more!

I would be nowhere without my editor Jeanette Shaw and my literary agent Wendy Sherman. Their belief in me, and in this book particularly, have helped me to expand my writing horizons and bring my message to more people. Both of these ladies are smart and kind and are full of the types of brilliant ideas (brought forth in a sincere and direct way) that make me so grateful they took a chance on this first-time author. I'm honored to work with them both.

Although I have never met them, I have been greatly influenced by a few radiant and luminous artists. I am so thankful for Bea Arthur, Bette Midler, Dolly Parton, Scott Bakula, and Julian Eltinge. They have taught me—by example—how to be me.

Amy Deneson and Kristina Villarini at GLSEN have advocated for my work for a long time. It makes me so happy to be associated with GLSEN because, as an organization, they diligently make schools safe for everyone. I am indeed #GLSENproud, because Amy and Kristina have been utterly gracious and welcoming and supportive of me and my message.

It is important to thank Mom and Dad. As a public figure, I've found that I can do the most help by honestly sharing my own story. When people hear what it was like to grow up as me, they find out that they are not alone. This process of sharing has sometimes come dangerously close to airing our family's dirty laundry. I am so grateful for two loving and accepting parents who are willing to support me in telling the whole story from my perspective, even when in that story they might seem to falter or not act exactly . . . heroically. Their willingness is, in itself, heroic to me. I love my parents and I am grateful for all of their love and support. I also thank my sister, Aileen, whose steady help and wise counsel about telling my story have been so valuable to me. And I am grateful for my brother, Mike, who offered help and understanding to me through some very tough years as a starving artist.

The intelligent and stunning Sarah Lohman has been a constant light and support during this process. How did I luck out with such a beautiful friend who was also writing her own opus, *Eight Flavors*, while I was writing this book? I am so happy to have had her love and faith and input and commiseration as I stumbled toward book launch. Adam Steinberg has been a true friend and a vivid example of a good person. I am forever in his debt for the way he has taught me to be an upright, generous, and considerate human being. And Rick Herron has taught me what makes a good friendship. We have grown together and Rick's constant trust and openhearted support have been priceless. I couldn't have asked for a better friend to walk through life with. Jacob Tobia is a great friend. I thank them for helping me continue to discover who I am and for the inspiration they give me to be open with everyone about me. I respect and appreciate the way they have helped me, and I'm so thankful for their work helping the genderqueer community.

Danny Coeyman is a true artist. He has brought so much kindness to these pages and to our long, long friendship. I am thankful that he was willing to brainstorm and connect with my words and honor and roll with my author process. I will always remember his open heart and mind as he began to bring to artistic life the words herein. He constantly makes me die laughing and helps me not take life so seriously. Like this book, his artworks and jokes go straight for the heart, and I'm so glad they do.

And now for the love of my life, Jeff . . . As far as this book goes, he has been my greatest supporter. Writing a book and telling your story is stressful and exhilarating, fearsome and freeing. And Jeff has been that perfect partner who has flowed and morphed with me all along the way—celebrating the highs and supporting the lows. As far as my life goes, it is a cliché to say that Jeff has taught me what love is. But without his example of loving me, I wouldn't have been able to make this book so clear and so rich. Have you ever had the experience of truly and unconditionally being seen and respected and loved? How could I ever express all the gratitude I have for that?

ABOUT THE AUTHOR

Author, host, and youth advocate Jeffrey Marsh has more than a quarter BILLION views across social media. As the creator of the global trends #DontSayThatsSoGay and #NoTimeToHateMyself, Jeffrey has earned spots on top Viner lists by both BuzzFeed and Vine with a positive, inclusive message. In 2015, Jeffrey was named official red carpet correspondent for both MTV/Logo and GLSEN and is a featured writer for *The Huffington Post* and *Medium*. Jeffrey is a precepted facilitator in the Soto Zen tradition of Buddhism, as well as a host, actor, singer, songwriter, dancer, and comedian.